GENESIS

Chapters 34—50

J. Vernon McGee

THOMAS NELSON PUBLISHERS

Nashville • Atlanta • London • Vancouver

Published in Nashville, Tennessee, by Thomas Nelson, Inc.

Scripture quotations are from the KING JAMES VERSION of the Bible.

Library of Congress Cataloging-in-Publication Data

McGee, J. Vernon (John Vernon), 1904–1988
    [Thru the Bible with J. Vernon McGee]
    Thru the Bible commentary series / J. Vernon McGee.
        p.   cm.
    Reprint. Originally published: Thru the Bible with J. Vernon McGee. 1975.
    Includes bibliographical references.
    ISBN 0-7852-1003-2 (TR)
    ISBN 0-7852-1069-5 (NRM)
    1. Bible—Commentaries. I. Title.
BS491.2.M37   1991
220.7′7—dc20   90-41340
                                                        CIP

Printed in the United States of America
7 8 9 — 99 98 97

CONTENTS

GENESIS—CHAPTERS 34—50

PREFACE

The radio broadcasts of the Thru the Bible Radio five-year program were transcribed, edited, and published first in single-volume paperbacks to accommodate the radio audience.

There has been a minimal amount of further editing for this publication. Therefore, these messages are not the word-for-word recording of the taped messages which went out over the air. The changes were necessary to accommodate a reading audience rather than a listening audience.

These are popular messages, prepared originally for a radio audience. They should not be considered a commentary on the entire Bible in any sense of that term. These messages are devoid of any attempt to present a theological or technical commentary on the Bible. Behind these messages is a great deal of research and study in order to interpret the Bible from a popular rather than from a scholarly (and too-often boring) viewpoint.

We have definitely and deliberately attempted "to put the cookies on the bottom shelf so that the kiddies could get them."

The fact that these messages have been translated into many languages for radio broadcasting and have been received with enthusiasm reveals the need for a simple teaching of the whole Bible for the masses of the world.

I am indebted to many people and to many sources for bringing this volume into existence. I should express my especial thanks to my secretary, Gertrude Cutler, who supervised the editorial work; to Dr. Elliott R. Cole, my associate, who handled all the detailed work with the publishers; and finally, to my wife Ruth for tenaciously encouraging me from the beginning to put my notes and messages into printed form.

Solomon wrote, ". . . of making many books there is no end; and much study is a weariness of the flesh" (Eccl. 12:12). On a sea of books that flood the marketplace, we launch this series of THRU THE BIBLE with the hope that it might draw many to the one Book, *The Bible*.

J. VERNON MCGEE

The Book of

GENESIS

INTRODUCTION

The Book of Genesis is one of the two important key books of the Bible. The book that opens the Old Testament (Genesis) and the book that opens the New Testament (Matthew) are the two books which I feel are the key to the understanding of the Scriptures.

Before beginning this study, I would like to suggest that you read the Book of Genesis through. It would be preferable to read it at one sitting. I recognize that this may be impossible for you to do, and if you want to know the truth, I have not been able to do it in one sitting. It has taken me several sittings because of interruptions. However, if you find it possible to read through Genesis at one sitting, you will find it very profitable.

Let me give you a bird's-eye view of Genesis, a view that will cover the total spectrum of the book. There are certain things that you should note because the Book of Genesis is, actually, germane to the entire Scripture. The fact of the matter is that Genesis is a book that states many things for the first time: creation, man, woman, sin, sabbath, marriage, family, labor, civilization, culture, murder, sacrifice, races, languages, redemption, and cities.

You will also find certain phrases that occur very frequently. For instance, "these are the generations of" is an important expression used frequently because the Book of Genesis gives the families of early history. That is important to us because we are members of the human family that begins here.

A number of very interesting characters are portrayed for us.

Someone has called this "the book of biographies." There are Abraham, Isaac, Jacob, Joseph, Pharaoh, and the eleven sons of Jacob besides Joseph. You will find that God is continually blessing Abraham, Isaac, Jacob, and Joseph. In addition, those who are associated with them—Lot, Abimelech, Potiphar, the butler, and Pharaoh—are also blessed of God.

In this book you will find mention of the covenant. There are frequent appearances of the Lord to the patriarchs, especially to Abraham. The altar is prominent in this book. Jealousy in the home is found here. Egypt comes before us in this book as it does nowhere else. The judgments upon sin are mentioned here, and there are evident leadings of Providence.

As we study, we need to keep in mind something that Browning wrote years ago in a grammarian's funeral essay: "Image the whole, then execute the parts. Fancy the fabric, quiet, e'er you build, e'er steel strike fire from quartz, e'er mortar dab brick." In other words, get the total picture of this book. I tell students that there are two ways of studying the Bible; one is with the telescope and the other way is with the microscope. At first, you need to get the telescopic view. After that, study it with a microscope.

A great preacher of the past, Robinson of England, has written something which I would like to write indelibly on the minds and hearts of God's people today:

We live in the age of books. They pour out for us from the press in an ever increasing multitude. And we are always reading manuals, textbooks, articles, books of devotion, books of criticism, books about the Bible, books about the Gospels, all are devoured with avidity. But what amount of time and labor do we give to the consideration of the Gospels themselves? We're constantly tempted to imagine that we get good more quickly by reading some modern statement of truth which we find comparatively easy to appropriate because it is presented to us in a shape, and from a standpoint, with which our education, or it may be partly association, has made us familiar. But the good we acquire readily is not that which enters most deeply into our being and becomes an abiding possession. It would be well if we could realize quite simply that nothing worth the having is to be gained without the winning. The great truths of nature are not offered to us in such a form as to make it easy to grasp them. The treasures of grace must be sought with all the skill and energy which are characteristic of the man who is searching for goodly pearls. (Robinson, *The Personal Life of the Clergy*.)

I love that statement because I believe that the Bible itself will speak to our hearts in a way that no other book can do. Therefore we have included the text of Scripture in this study. New translations are appearing in our day; in fact, they are coming from the presses as fast and prolifically as rabbits multiply. However, I will continue to use the Authorized or King James Version. I refuse to substitute the pungency of genius with the bland, colorless, and tasteless mediocrity of the present day.

MAJOR DIVISIONS OF THE BOOK

Where would you divide the Book of Genesis if you divided it into two parts? Notice that the first eleven chapters constitute a whole and that, beginning with chapter 12 through the remainder of the book, we find an altogether different section. The two parts differ in several ways: The first section extends from creation to Abraham. The second section extends from Abraham through Joseph. The first section deals with major *subjects*, subjects which still engage the minds of thoughtful men in our day: the Creation, the Fall, the Flood, the Tower of Babel. The second section has to do with personalities: Abraham, the man of faith; Isaac, the beloved son; Jacob, the chosen and chastened son; and Joseph, his suffering and glory.

Although that is a major division, there is another division even more significant. It has to do with *time*. The first eleven chapters cover a minimum time span of two thousand years—actually, two thousand years *plus*. I feel that it is safe to say that they may cover several hundred thousand years. I believe this first section of Genesis can cover any time in the past that you may need to fit into your particular theory, and the chances are that you would come short of it even then. At least we know the book covers a minimum of two thousand years in the first eleven chapters, but the second section of thirty-nine chapters covers only three hundred and fifty years. In fact, beginning with Genesis 12 and running all the way through the Old Testament and the New Testament, a total time span of only two thousand years is covered. Therefore, as far as *time* is concerned, you are halfway through the Bible when you cover the first eleven chapters of Genesis.

This should suggest to your mind and heart that God had some definite purpose in giving this first section to us. Do you think that God is putting the emphasis on this first section or on the rest of the Bible? Isn't it evident that He is putting the emphasis on the last part? The first section has to do with the universe and with creation, but the last part deals with man, with nations, and with the person of Jesus Christ. God was more interested in Abraham than He was in the entire created universe. And, my friend, God is more interested in you and attaches more value to you than He does to the entire physical universe.

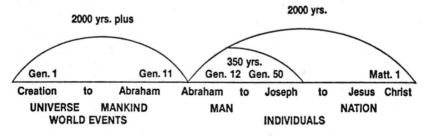

Let me further illustrate this. Of the eighty-nine chapters in the four Gospel records, only four chapters cover the first thirty years of the life of the Lord Jesus while eighty-five chapters cover the last three years of His life, and twenty-seven chapters cover the final eight *days* of His life. Where does that indicate that the Spirit of God is placing the emphasis? I am sure you will agree that the emphasis is on the last part, the last eight days covered by the twenty-seven chapters. And what is that all about? It's about the death, burial, and resurrection of the Lord Jesus Christ. That is the important part of the Gospel record. In other words, God has given the Gospels that you might believe that Christ died for our sins and that He was raised for our justification. That is essential. That is the all-important truth.

May I say that the first eleven chapters of Genesis are merely the introduction to the Bible, and we need to look at them in this fashion. This does not mean that we are going to pass over the first eleven chapters. Actually, we will spend quite a bit of time with them.

Genesis is the "seed plot" of the Bible, and here we find the beginning, the source, the birth of everything. The Book of Genesis is just like the bud of a beautiful rose, and it opens out into the rest of the Bible. The truth here is in germ form.

One of the best divisions which can be made of the Book of Genesis is according to the genealogies—i.e., according to the families.

Gen. 1—2:6	Book of Generations of Heavens and Earth
Gen. 2:7—6:8	Book of Generations of Adam
Gen. 6:9—9:29	Generations of Noah
Gen. 10:1—11:9	Generations of Sons of Noah
Gen. 11:10-26	Generations of Sons of Shem
Gen. 11:27—25:11	Generations of Terah
Gen. 25:12-18	Generations of Ishmael
Gen. 25:19—35:29	Generations of Isaac
Gen. 36:1—37:1	Generations of Esau
Gen. 37:2—50:26	Generations of Jacob

All of these are given to us in the Book of Genesis. It is a book of families. Genesis is an amazing book, and it will help us to look at it from this viewpoint.

OUTLINE

CHAPTER 34

THEME: Dinah defiled by Shechem; Simeon and Levi slay the men of Hamor

Frankly, Jacob made a mistake by stopping in Shalem, for there is going to be a scandal at this point in the family of this man. Dinah, the daughter of Jacob by Leah, is defiled by Shechem, son of Hamor the Hivite. Then Simeon and Levi, Dinah's full brothers, avenge this act by slaying all the inhabitants of the city of Hamor. This cannot be justified, and it is a dark blot on the family of Jacob. It reveals the fact that Jacob did not get away too soon when he left his Uncle Laban down in the land of Haran. We need to see that God was right in getting him away from that environment.

There are two things that God spends a great deal of time with in Genesis. First of all, there is heredity. God is very much concerned that a believer marry a believer and that a believer not marry an unbeliever. That is important for the sake of heredity. The second thing of concern is the environment of the individual. We see this especially in the life of Jacob. He has a big family. Not only were there twelve sons, but there were also daughters. We are given the record of only this one daughter because she features in this very sad chapter.

There is something else for us to note that is important to the understanding of Genesis, and that is that there is trouble in the families. Have you noticed that? There was strife and trouble in the family of Abraham. There was strife and trouble in the family of Isaac. Esau was Isaac's favorite, and Rebekah's favorite was her son Jacob—and that caused a great deal of trouble in the family. Now we will see that there was a great deal of trouble in the family of Jacob.

Jacob stops and stays in Shalem for awhile, and it is going to cause a great deal of sorrow to him. Very frankly, chapter 34 is a sad, sordid chapter, and this must have been a heartbreak to old Jacob at this time. Jacob (or Israel, as we should call him) has built an altar, and he is now giving a testimony to the living and true God. There is a change in his life, but it is a slow growth, a development. This should be a lesson to us today: Don't expect that, as a Christian, you are going to become full grown overnight. God adopts us as full-grown sons into the family where we are able to understand the divine truth because the Holy Spirit is our Teacher. But our spiritual growth and our progress are very slow. We may learn truths in the Bible, but we will find that in our lives we are very much like Simon Peter, stumbling here and falling down there. Thank God that Simon Peter kept getting up and brushing himself off, and there came a day when he had a very close walk with the Lord. In fact, he walked to a cross even as our Lord did. You and I need to recognize that in our own lives the growth is slow, and therefore the growth in others will also be slow. Sometimes parents of converted children expect too much of them. Let's not expect too much of other folk, but let's also expect a great deal of ourselves.

There are three chapters in the Book of Genesis that are not pretty at all, and they all concern the children of Leah, the elder daughter of Laban who was given to Jacob. I believe that this gives evidence of the fact that God does not approve of plurality of marriages. The very fact that it was forced on Jacob to a certain extent did not make it right, by any means—Jacob at least went along with it. We find in this section that the children of Leah are all involved in sin. She had four boys. In this chapter it is Simeon and Levi. In chapter 35 we come to another of the sons, Reuben, the firstborn. In chapter 38 it will be Judah. Every one of Leah's sons turned out rather badly, and there was flagrant sin in their lives.

We have already noted that there was a great deal of strife in all of these families, but now another element has entered in. There is sordidness and a shoddiness that has seeped into the family of Jacob that was not in the family of Abraham or of Isaac. They had a great deal of difficulty and many problems, but nothing like we see in Jacob's family. Again, God wanted to get this man Jacob and his family out from the home of Laban, out from that atmosphere, because the very atmosphere gave the background for these awful sins that are mentioned here.

DINAH DEFILED BY SHECHEM

Jacob has stopped here at Shalem and has bought himself a nice little place out in the surburban area of town. He is attempting, as it were, to orient himself to the culture of that day. Well, it wasn't a good place, and God wants to separate this man from this area also. And believe me, after you read this chapter you will come to the conclusion that God had *better* separate him from it!

> And Dinah the daughter of Leah, which she bare unto Jacob, went out to see the daughters of the land [Gen. 34:1].

Dinah went visiting in this town of Shalem.

> And when Shechem the son of Hamor the Hivite, prince of the country, saw her, he took her, and lay with her, and defiled her [Gen. 34:2].

Let me put it in the language of the news media today: He raped her. If they can say it in print and on radio and television, certainly this poor preacher can say it. Sin needs to be spelled out. There was a time when sin was sin, but now they've taken the "s" off of it, and you're in the "in" group if you're a sinner. But that's not the way God spells sin. He still spells it S-I-N. And you will notice that "I" is right in the middle of the word—that's where all of us are.

> And his soul clave unto Dinah the daughter of Jacob, and he loved the damsel, and spake kindly unto the damsel.
>
> And Shechem spake unto his father Hamor, saying, Get me this damsel to wife [Gen. 34:3–4].

The very interesting thing is that the boy Shechem was apparently in love with the girl and really wanted to marry her.

> And Jacob heard that he had defiled Dinah his daughter:
> now his sons were with his cattle in the field: and Jacob
> held his peace until they were come.
>
> And Hamor the father of Shechem went out unto Jacob to
> commune with him.
>
> And the sons of Jacob came out of the field when they
> heard it: and the men were grieved, and they were very
> wroth, because he had wrought folly in Israel in lying
> with Jacob's daughter; which thing ought not to be done
> [Gen. 34:5-7].

We certainly agree that it should not have been done, but it had been,
and now the fellow wants to marry her. When Jacob heard it, he waited
for his boys to come in, and they had a war counsel. I am of the opinion that Jacob probably should not have made as much of it as he did.
When Hamor, the father of Shechem, came out to him, it is obvious
that he wanted to get the girl for his son's wife. Jacob probably should
have yielded to that, because that was, shall I say, the best way out at
the time. Certainly, the way it was handled was not the best by any
means, and God did not approve of it.

> And Hamor communed with them, saying, The soul of
> my son Shechem longeth for your daughter: I pray you
> give her him to wife.
>
> And make ye marriages with us, and give your daugh-
> ters unto us, and take our daughters unto you [Gen.
> 34:8-9].

Although intermarriage would have been wrong, it seems that Dinah
should have been given to Shechem because that would have prevented a worse sin. This, of course, is hindsight, and "Monday morning quarterbacks" are not always right.

> And ye shall dwell with us: and the land shall be before

you; dwell and trade ye therein, and get you possessions therein.

And Shechem said unto her father and unto her brethren, Let me find grace in your eyes, and what ye shall say unto me I will give.

Ask me never so much dowry and gift, and I will give according as ye shall say unto me: but give me the damsel to wife [Gen. 34:10–12].

All of this reveals that Jacob is going to have to move on. This is no place for him, mixing with these people in this land.

And the sons of Jacob answered Shechem and Hamor his father deceitfully, and said, because he had defiled Dinah their sister [Gen. 34:13].

I feel that Jacob should certainly have taken the leadership in his family. First of all, he should have prevented his sons from deceiving Shechem and Hamor.

And they said unto them, We cannot do this thing, to give our sister to one that is uncircumcised; for that were a reproach unto us [Gen. 34:14].

The thing that disturbs me about this incident is that the real reproach—the sin of rape—is ignored, and they make the reproach on the basis of the rule which God had given them regarding intermarriage with the uncircumcised.

But in this will we consent unto you: If ye will be as we be, that every male of you be circumcised;

Then will we give our daughters unto you, and we will take your daughters to us, and we will dwell with you, and we will become one people.

**But if ye will not hearken unto us, to be circumcised;
then will we take our daughter, and we will be gone
[Gen. 34:15–17].**

The thing that Jacob's sons ask them to do is to go through the ritual of circumcision.

This ought to be a warning today to a great many people. I recall one couple who came to me for counseling and asked me to perform their marriage ceremony. I would not unite them in marriage because he was not a Christian, and she claimed that she would not marry him unless he became a Christian. I talked with him, and he said he would accept Christ. We had prayer, and then I asked him, "What have you really done?" I have never heard such hemming and hawing and beating around the bush as this boy did. Very frankly, I said right in front of him, "Young lady, I'll not perform the ceremony. I don't think the young man is converted." They felt that I was being very harsh, and they went down the street and got another preacher to perform the ceremony. After they were married, she tried to get him to go to church. Of course, he had a good reason for not coming to hear me preach because I'd been so cruel to him, but then she agreed to go to another church, and they went two or three times. Finally, he just said to her point-blank, "Really, I'm not a Christian." Just to go through the ceremony of joining the church and even of saying you trust Christ doesn't mean you have. I find that faith doesn't seem to mean very much to a great many people today. They think it is enough just to nod your head. It is a tremendous experience, my friend, to trust Christ as your Savior. There's nothing quite like it, nothing to compare to it in this world. When you trust Christ as Savior, it does something for you. It didn't do anything for that boy.

Mark Twain had the same experience. He was not a Christian, and he was in love with a very beautiful, wonderful Christian girl. She would not marry him until he became a Christian. He professed to have accepted Christ as his Savior, and they started out their marriage that way. Well, Mark Twain became very famous, and he was entertained by many famous people in the world. One day when he came back to his home in Missouri and she wanted to go to church, he said,

"Look, I can't keep up the front any longer. You go on to church. I know now that I'm not a Christian." May I say that made a very unhappy home, and it absolutely spoiled the life of this lovely Christian girl.

Here the sons of Jacob are saying, "If you'll go through the rite of circumcision, it will make everything all right." A great many people think that if you join the church, nod your head, and are able to use the right vocabulary and quote the right verse, that means you are a Christian. My friend, that does not mean you are a Christian. If you have trusted in Christ, something has happened, and you are a different person.

> And their words pleased Hamor, and Shechem Hamor's son.
>
> And the young man deferred not to do the thing, because he had delight in Jacob's daughter: and he was more honourable than all the house of his father [Gen. 34:18–19].

I agree that this boy is doing the honorable thing at this point.

> And Hamor and Shechem his son came unto the gate of their city, and communed with the men of their city, saying,
>
> These men are peaceable with us; therefore let them dwell in the land, and trade therein; for the land, behold, it is large enough for them; let us take their daughters to us for wives, and let us give them our daughters.
>
> Only herein will the men consent unto us for to dwell with us, to be one people, if every male among us be circumcised, as they are circumcised.
>
> Shall not their cattle and their substance and every beast of theirs be ours? only let us consent unto them, and they will dwell with us [Gen. 34:20–23].

In other words, through intermarriage these men expected to eventually own everything that Jacob had.

> **And unto Hamor and unto Shechem his son hearkened all that went out of the gate of his city; and every male was circumcised, all that went out of the gate of his city [Gen. 34:24].**

Performing the rite of circumcision on unbelievers was as phony as it could be. It is like joining a church when you are unconverted.

SIMEON AND LEVI SLAY THE MEN OF HAMOR

> **And it came to pass on the third day, when they were sore, that two of the sons of Jacob, Simeon and Levi, Dinah's brethren, took each man his sword, and came upon the city boldly, and slew all the males [Gen. 34:25].**

This was real trickery. Simeon and Levi were Dinah's full brothers, and they wanted to get revenge. In their revenge, they go too far. Neither the rape nor the fact that Hamor intended to dispossess Jacob and his sons of the great wealth which Jacob had accumulated in Haran can in any way justify the brutal act of Simeon and Levi, but it does reveal the impossible situation of dealing with the inhabitants of that land. The thing they have done is a very terrible thing.

> **And they slew Hamor and Shechem his son with the edge of the sword, and took Dinah out of Shechem's house, and went out.**
>
> **The sons of Jacob came upon the slain, and spoiled the city, because they had defiled their sister [Gen. 34:26–27].**

The other sons joined in on this. This reveals greed in the family of
Jacob that is not right and which they had learned in the home of
Laban.

> **They took their sheep, and their oxen, and their asses,
> and that which was in the city, and that which was in
> the field,**
>
> **And all their wealth, and all their little ones, and their
> wives took they captive, and spoiled even all that was in
> the house.**
>
> **And Jacob said to Simeon and Levi, Ye have troubled me
> to make me to stink among the inhabitants of the land,
> among the Canaanites and the Perizzites: and I being
> few in number, they shall gather themselves together
> against me, and slay me; and I shall be destroyed, I and
> my house [Gen. 34:28–30].**

Notice something that is obviously wrong here in the life of Jacob.
Jacob rebukes Simeon and Levi for giving him a bad name, but he
doesn't rebuke them for the sin that they have committed. We sometimes get a wrong perspective of sin and of our actions. We think only
of the *effect* that it is going to have. There are many men and women in
our churches who will not take a stand on certain issues. Why? Well,
the little crowd they run with may not accept them. They are with a
little clique, and they don't dare stand for anything that the little
clique wouldn't stand for. It is never a question of whether it is right or
wrong; it's a question of whether it ingratiates them to the crowd. God
have mercy on Christians who shape their lives by those who are
around them and who are constantly looking for the effect their conduct is going to have on others. They do not look on whether this is the
right thing or the Christian thing or whether as a child of God this is
something they should or should not do. This is the reason our
churches are filled with those who compromise, and it is little wonder
that we have so many frustrated, unhappy Christians today. It is a

wonderful thing to stand for the truth, and when you stand for it, then you don't have to compromise. How wonderful it is when we will do that. Poor old Jacob is growing, but he hasn't grown that far.

Then these boys, of course, attempt to defend themselves:

And they said, Should he deal with our sister as with an harlot? [Gen. 34:31].

That's a good question. I would say that if they wanted to take the judgment into their own hands, they first of all should have heard this boy out and let him marry their sister. It would have been the best thing to do under the circumstances, but it is not the right thing, by any means. Certainly that would have been better than to go to the extreme of murdering the inhabitants of that land. There is no excuse that can be offered, and I have no defense to offer for them at all. They should not have done the thing that they did, but we must understand that they were not living in the light of Romans 12:19–21 which says: "Dearly beloved, avenge not yourselves, but rather give place unto wrath: for it is written, Vengeance is mine; I will repay, saith the Lord. Therefore if thine enemy hunger, feed him; if he thirst, give him drink: for in so doing thou shalt heap coals of fire on his head. Be not overcome of evil, but overcome evil with good." For a Christian today Romans 12 is the policy that he should follow. The very minute we attempt to take revenge or get vengeance, it means that we are no longer walking by faith. We are saying that we cannot trust God to work it out. However, I am not sure that you could bring Jacob—and certainly not his sons—up to such a spiritual level at that particular time. But you cannot justify this terrible deed which they have committed. You can well understand that they acted because of their feeling for their sister and the shame which had been brought upon the family. Jacob was beginning to see that a whole lot of chickens—not just a few—were coming home to roost.

CHAPTER 35

THEME: Jacob returns to Bethel; God renews the covenant; Rachel dies at the birth of Benjamin; death of Isaac

After the study in chapter 34, you may have come to the conclusion that I made a blunder when I said that Jacob's life changed at Peniel. Actually, we did not see too much change in what took place in the thirty-fourth chapter. That is quite true, but there was a change that took place. I hesitate to call Jacob's experience at Peniel a crisis experience because I am afraid that this matter of a crisis experience has been overdrawn by a great many. There are some folk who feel that if you don't have a second experience, you just haven't had anything. The fact of the matter is that that's not true. Some have a wonderful crisis experience, and I'm sure that many of us can turn back to that in our lives. But there are those who cannot or do not and have never mentioned it as being something very important in their lives. But when Jacob came to Peniel, a tremendous thing happened to him. All the way from the beginning of the life of Jacob until Peniel, his life was characterized by the rise of self, the assertion of the flesh—that's Jacob and nothing but that. What really happened at Peniel was the fall of self. He went down like a deflated tire. He had been pumped up like a balloon, and he went down to practically nothing. But actually, chapter 34 evidences that he was not yet walking by faith.

As soon as Esau had turned his back and started home, Jacob took his family down to Shalem. It is a tragic move. Jacob was still depending upon his own cleverness. Dinah was raped, and Simeon and Levi, her full brothers, went into the city of Shalem to the prince who was responsible. Although he wanted to marry her, they murdered him, and the sons of Jacob conducted a slaughter that would make a gang shooting in Chicago look pretty tame. When they came home, Jacob said, "You have made my name to smell among the people of my land."

Many expositors say that it was a tragic thing for Jacob to stop in Shalem, and I must say that I have to go along with that partially. But I have one question to ask: Was Jacob ready for Bethel? Was he ready for the experiences that God was going to give him? No, I think that the tragic things that took place in chapter 34 were the result of a man who had been walking in the energy of the flesh. There had been a deflation of self, but there was no discernible faith in God. Because he did not have faith to go on to Bethel, he stopped at Shalem. These tragic things which took place in his life reveal that this man was not a leader in his own family. He was not taking the proper place that he should have. He was no spiritual giant, by any means. And to have those eleven boys to herd was really a job for which this man Jacob was not prepared. After this tragic event, Jacob now is beginning to see the hand of God in his life, and now he makes the decision that he probably should have made beforehand.

JACOB RETURNS TO BETHEL

And God said unto Jacob, Arise, go up to Beth-el, and dwell there: and make there an altar unto God, that appeared unto thee when thou fleddest from the face of Esau thy brother [Gen. 35:1].

Now God is calling this man back to Bethel. After this sad experience, he is prepared to go. You see, he didn't have faith to move out before, but Jacob now begins to take the spiritual leadership in his home.

Then Jacob said unto his household, and to all that were with him, Put away the strange gods that are among you, and be clean, and change your garments [Gen. 35:2].

There are several things that Jacob tells his household to do. First of all, they are to "put away the strange gods that are among you." We are almost shocked at this. You will recall that when Jacob fled with Rachel and Leah, Rachel slipped out with the family gods. Apparently, she had sat on them while riding the camel—she just crawled on top of the luggage that was on the camel's back and sat down because these little images were underneath. Jacob did not know at the time that she had taken them. He was very honest when he told Laban that the images were not in his entourage at all. That may have been one of the few times he was truthful with Laban. He really had not known they were there.

When they were discovered, I think that we would all assume that Jacob would get rid of them because he knew of the living and true God. In fact, he had had a personal encounter with Him. But he didn't get rid of the images, and now we find that his entire family is worshiping these strange gods. For the first time, Jacob is the one to take the spiritual leadership, and he says, "Let's get rid of these false gods, these strange gods." The first thing they have to do is to put away that which is wrong.

There are too many folk who six days a week are serving some other god, and on Sunday they try to serve the Lord. Many Christians, even fundamental believers, have their strange gods, and then they wonder why their service in church on Sunday is not a thrilling experience. My friend, you are going to have to put away your strange gods. I don't know what yours might be. It could be covetousness. There is many a good fundamental businessman who is out after every dollar he can get. He gives more devotion to getting the dollar than he does to serving the Lord on Sunday. And then he wonders what is wrong with his spiritual life. If you are going to come back to Bethel where you met God at the beginning, then, my friend, you must put away those things that are wrong.

Then Jacob says, "Be clean." For the believer, that means confession of sins. You have to deal with sin in your life. You cannot come to church on Sunday and dismiss the way you have lived during the week that has just passed. After all, you take a physical bath and use a deodorant before you come to church, and yet there is spiritual body odor in our churches because there is no confession of sin, no cleansing. "If we confess our sins, he is faithful and just to forgive our sins, and to cleanse us from all unrighteousness" (1 John 1:9). There must be the confession. He will forgive, but we must confess.

"And change your garments." In other words, get rid of the old garments. In Scripture "garments" speak of habits. We speak of an equestrian wearing a riding habit or of a football player wearing a uniform—which is his habit. In like manner, the child of God should dress in a way to mirror who he is and to whom he belongs. Do you wear the habits of the Lord? Can you be detected in business or in school or in the neighborhood as being a little different in your life? You *are* wearing a habit. The day that Jacob went back to Bethel, he started living for God. Up to then, I don't think he was. Now he says, "Let's go back to Bethel"—that's the thing that we must do.

> **And let us arise, and go up to Beth-el; and I will make there an altar unto God, who answered me in the day of my distress, and was with me in the way which I went [Gen. 35:3].**

Abraham and Isaac had made altars, and now Jacob will make an altar—thank God for that. He will now have a witness for God.

"Who answered me in the day of my distress, and was with me in the way which I went." The thing that Jacob remembered is that when he was running away from home as a young man, homesick and lonesome, he had come to Bethel, and God had been faithful to him. God had said, "I will be faithful to you." The years had gone by, and God certainly had been faithful to him. Now God says, "You've got to go back to Bethel. You have to go back to where you started. You have to begin there."

We need to recognize that the years we spend in living a shoddy, shabby Christian life are a waste of time, absolutely a waste of time. God called the children of Israel to get out of Egypt and into the land of promise. God appeared to them and told them to go into the land, but they didn't go in. Forty years they wandered around, and then God appeared to Joshua and said, "Go into the land." He picked up right where He had left off. They had wasted forty years. How many people are wasting their lives as Christians? My, the tremendous spiritual lessons that are here for us! I don't know about you, but some of us are just like Jacob, and that's the reason this is so applicable to us today. Thank God that He says He is the God of Jacob. I love that! If He'll be the God of Jacob, He'll be the God of J. Vernon McGee also—that's wonderful! This chapter is a great encouragement to us.

Notice that Jacob is assuming authority in his home.

> **And they gave unto Jacob all the strange gods which were in their hand, and all their earrings which were in their ears; and Jacob hid them under the oak which was by Shechem [Gen. 35:4].**

Let me pause to say that earrings were associated with worship in that day—there is a great deal said in Scripture about that. The earrings identified them as idolaters, and so they are going to get rid of them.

"Jacob hid them under the oak which was by Shechem." Jacob got rid of them. They're not stored away—they're buried. They must be put away because it is now going to be a new life.

> **And they journeyed: and the terror of God was upon the cities that were round about them, and they did not pursue after the sons of Jacob.**

> **So Jacob came to Luz, which is in the land of Canaan, that is, Beth-el, he and all the people that were with him [Gen. 35:5–6].**

This place was called Luz before Jacob changed the name to Bethel, and the people in that day knew it as Luz, not as Bethel. We know it today as Bethel.

> **And he built there an altar, and called the place El-beth-el: because there God appeared unto him, when he fled from the face of his brother [Gen. 35:7].**

Beth-el, meaning "the house of God," was the name that Jacob had given to it before. Now he called it *El-Beth-el*, which means "*God* of the house of God." This reveals spiritual growth in Jacob's life.

Now here is a very interesting sidelight:

> **But Deborah Rebekah's nurse died, and she was buried beneath Beth-el under an oak: and the name of it was called Allon-bachuth [Gen. 35:8].**

Since Deborah was with Jacob at this time, we assume that Rebekah had already died, and Scripture does not tell us when her death took place. Poor Jacob never saw his mother again. That part is not as tragic as the fact that she never saw him again—she had just sent him away for a little while, you know. The nurse apparently had brought a message of Rebekah's death and had come to stay with Jacob—and now she dies.

GOD RENEWS THE COVENANT

> **And God appeared unto Jacob again, when he came out of Padan-aram, and blessed him [Gen. 35:9].**

All those years God had been trying to deal with Jacob. Now he picks up right where He had met him when he came to Bethel as a young man. Those years he spent down there with Uncle Laban, in many ways, were wasted years.

> **And God said unto him, Thy name is Jacob: thy name shall not be called any more Jacob, but Israel shall be thy name: and he called his name Israel.**

> **And God said unto him, I am God Almighty: be fruitful and multiply; a nation and a company of nations shall be of thee, and kings shall come out of thy loins [Gen. 35:10–11].**

"I am God Almighty." Remember that that is what He had told Abraham.

> **And the land which I gave Abraham and Isaac, to thee I
> will give it, and to thy seed after thee will I give the land
> [Gen. 35:12].**

The Lord considers that pretty important property, by the way. This now is the third time He has promised them the land—first to Abraham, then to Isaac, and now to Jacob. The Lord had to tell each one of these men about it two or three times; in fact, He told Abraham many times.

> **And God went up from him in the place where he talked
> with him.**
>
> **And Jacob set up a pillar in the place where he talked
> with him, even a pillar of stone; and he poured a drink
> offering thereon, and he poured oil thereon.**
>
> **And Jacob called the name of the place where God
> spake with him, Beth-el [Gen. 35:13–15].**

Here is the first mention of a drink offering. In the Book of Leviticus, five offerings are given, but not a drink offering. In fact, no instruction is given about it at all, but it is mentioned. Evidently this is one of the oldest offerings, and it has a very wonderful meaning to the believer today. The drink offering was just poured on the other offerings, and it went up in the steam. Paul told the Philippians that that is the way he wanted his life to be—just poured out like a drink offering.

RACHEL DIES AT THE BIRTH OF BENJAMIN

> **And they journeyed from Beth-el; and there was but a
> little way to come to Ephrath: and Rachel travailed, and
> she had hard labour [Gen. 35:16].**

Rachel had one son Joseph, but now she has a second son.

> **And it came to pass, when she was in hard labour, that the midwife said unto her, Fear not; thou shalt have this son also.**
>
> **And it came to pass, as her soul was in departing, (for she died) that she called his name Ben-oni: but his father called him Benjamin [Gen. 35:17-18].**

What a wonderful thing this is—not the death of Rachel, but the way this took place. She says, "Call him 'son of my sorrow,'" but Jacob looked down at him and said, "I've lost my lovely Rachel, and this little fellow looks like her, so I'll just call him Benjamin, 'son of my right hand.'" Jacob was partial to the sons of Rachel.

Jacob's love for Rachel was perhaps the only fine thing in his life during those years in Padan-aram when there was so much evidence of the flesh and of self-seeking. He loved Rachel—there is no question about that. He was totally devoted to her. He was willing to do almost anything for her, such as permitting her to keep the images she had taken from her father. I don't think that Leah would have gotten by with it—or anyone else for that matter. But he was indulgent with Rachel. She had given Jacob his son Joseph, and now she gives birth to Benjamin. And it was at the birth of her second son that she died. His life meant her death. It was a great heartbreak to Jacob.

The other ten boys were no joy to him at all. God reminded him, I think, every day for twenty-four hours of the day that it was sinful to have more than one wife. He didn't need all of them. However, God will overrule, of course. (And He overrules in your life and mine. We can thank Him for that!) But the facts reveal that God did not approve of this plural marriage. This is especially obvious in the treatment which Joseph received from his half-brothers.

Jacob loved Joseph and Benjamin and, very frankly, the other boys were jealous of that. He should not have shown such partiality to Joseph because he had experienced the results of partiality in his own home—he had been the one whom his father had more or less pushed aside. He knew the trouble it had caused. Although I don't try to defend Jacob, we can sympathize with him. He had lost his lovely Rachel, but he had Benjamin. While it was true that the boy was the son of Rachel's sorrow, Jacob could not call him Benoni. He was not the reason of *his* sorrow; he was the son of his right hand, his walking stick, his staff, the one he would lean on in his old age. It is important to recognize this because it will help us understand the great sorrow Jacob will go through later on. All of it will have its roots in Jacob's sin. God does not approve of the wrong in our lives, my friend. We think we can get by with it, but we will not get by with it—anymore than Jacob got by with it.

And Rachel died, and was buried in the way to Ephrath, which is Beth-lehem [Gen. 35:19].

She is buried there today. I have several pictures that I have taken of her tomb that is there.

And Jacob set a pillar upon her grave: that is the pillar of Rachel's grave unto this day [Gen. 35:20].

That is, it was there until the time Moses wrote this, but it is also there to this very day.

And Israel journeyed, and spread his tent beyond the tower of Edar [Gen. 35:21].

In verses 22–26 we have a listing of the sons of Jacob by his different wives. Actually, Joseph and Benjamin were the two boys that were outstanding. The others just didn't turn out well. Again, this proves the fact that God does not bless a plurality of wives. The family of Jacob ought to illustrate that fact to us. Although Uncle Laban was responsible, of course, Jacob went along with it.

DEATH OF ISAAC

And Isaac gave up the ghost, and died, and was gathered unto his people, being old and full of days: and his sons Esau and Jacob buried him [Gen. 35:29].

I suspect that the death of their father Isaac was the only occasion which brought these two boys together in the years following Jacob's return to the land.

Have you noticed that this chapter is made prominent by death? First there is the death of Deborah, the maid of Rebekah. In this there is the suggestion of the death of Rebekah herself. Then there is the death of lovely Rachel. Finally, the chapter closes with the death of Isaac.

CHAPTER 36

THEME: Esau moves from Canaan to Mount Seir

This chapter deals entirely with the family of Esau which became the nation of Edom. Although it may not be too interesting for the average reader, it is a marvelous study for one who wants to follow through on these names and the peoples who came from them. You will find that some of the names mentioned here are names that one hears out on that great Arabian desert today. Omar, the tentmaker, belongs out there, as do Teman and Zepho and Kenaz and Korah. Well, here is the family of Esau, and they are still located out in that area.

The family of Esau settled in Edom, which is right south and east of the Dead Sea. It is a mountainous area, and the capital of Edom, the rock-hewn city of Petra, stands there today. Prophecy in the books of Isaiah, Jeremiah, Ezekiel, and Obadiah concerning Edom has been remarkably fulfilled.

The nation of Edom came from Esau. Three times in this chapter it is made very clear that Esau is the father of Edom—in fact, the names are synonymous (notice verse 8, for example). Then what is the difference between Esau and Edom? Well, when we first met Esau, we saw him as a boy in the family of Isaac. He was the outdoor, rugged type, a fine-looking athletic boy, by the way. Outwardly, he looked attractive, but if there ever was a man of the flesh, Esau was that man.

Years ago a Christian girl talked to me about a fine-looking young man whom she had met. To tell the truth, they were both fine-looking young people. She had been born in China. Her father was in the oil business and had been made very wealthy. She met this young man who was a bank clerk, a very poor boy. I had been a bank clerk when I was a young fellow, and I knew that a lot of bank clerks look around for a good marriage. They notice the daughters of customers who have money in the bank. So this boy had met the girl. He was a handsome brute, fine-looking, the rugged type. To me he looked like Esau. She was a lovely Christian girl who had been led to the Lord by a missionary while in China. She insisted on marrying this young man, hoping that he would come to the Lord. I had talked with him and knew he had no notion of coming to the Lord, but he wanted to marry that girl. She was beautiful and she had money—and he was a man of flesh. I told them I could not perform the ceremony. She was quite provoked with me, but later on she came back to tell me that she was divorced. She told me she had never known a person so given over to the things that were secular and carnal and of the flesh. She said she never dreamed there could be a person who would never in his entire life have a high, noble, spiritual, wonderful thought. She said he was as crude as one could possibly be. On the surface he gave a good impression, and he had been well mannered and chivalrous when they were courting, but underneath the facade he was crude and rude. Well, that is Esau, also. If you had been an attractive young lady in Esau's day and had seen him there in his family, the chances are that you would have been glad to date him. He was an attractive young man, but he was a man of the flesh.

Perhaps someone will want to argue with God about His choice of Jacob over Esau. Esau looked so good on the outside. Could God have made a mistake? Well, over in the little prophecy of Obadiah we see Esau unveiled. One little Esau has become about one hundred thousand Edomites. Each one of them is a little Esau. Now take a look at the nation and you will see what came from Esau. It is like putting Esau under a microscope; he is greatly enlarged. What do we see? We see a nation filled with pride. God said to Edom: "The pride of thine heart hath deceived thee, thou that dwellest in the clefts of the rock, whose habitation is high; that saith in his heart, Who shall bring me down to the ground? Though thou exalt thyself as the eagle, and though thou set thy nest among the stars, thence will I bring thee down, saith the Lord" (Obad. 1:3–4). The pride of their heart was a declaration of independence, a soul that says it can live without God and does not have a need for God. That is Esau.

In the last book of the Old Testament God says, "Jacob have I loved and Esau have I hated." God never said that until over one thousand years after these men lived, but God knew the heart of Esau at the beginning. After they worked their way out in history, it is obvious to us all that God was accurate.

> **Now these are the generations of Esau, who is Edom [Gen. 36:1].**

Again we are told that Esau is Edom.

> **Esau took his wives of the daughters of Canaan; Adah the daughter of Elon the Hittite, and Aholibamah the daughter of Anah the daughter of Zibeon the Hivite;**
>
> **And Bashemath Ishmael's daughter, sister of Nebajoth [Gen. 36:2–3].**

Esau, you recall, had married two Canaanite women and also an Ishmaelite woman.

> **And Esau took his wives, and his sons, and his daughters, and all the persons of his house, and his cattle, and all his beasts, and all his substance, which he had got in the land of Canaan; and went into the country from the face of his brother Jacob.**
>
> **For their riches were more than that they might dwell together; and the land wherein they were strangers could not bear them because of their cattle [Gen. 36:6–7].**

Remember that Abraham and Lot had had that same problem. There was not enough grazing land for them. Each one had too many cattle. They had separated and now Esau leaves the Promised Land, leaves it on his own, due to economic circumstances.

> **Thus dwelt Esau in mount Seir: Esau is Edom [Gen. 36:8].**

Now Esau moves from "the land of Seir" in Canaan, where he lived
when Jacob returned from Padan-aram (Gen. 32:3), to Mount Seir,
which I have already described.

> **And Timna was concubine to Eliphaz Esau's son; and
> she bare to Eliphaz Amalek: these were the sons of Adah
> Esau's wife [Gen. 36:12].**

This is the beginning of the Amalekites. Down through the centuries
those tribes which were there in the desert pushed out in many direc-
tions. Many of them pushed across North Africa. All the Arab tribes
came from Abraham—through Hagar, the Egyptian, and through Keturah, whom he married after the death of Sarah. And there has been
intermarriage between the tribes. They belong to the same family that
Israelites belong to.

In the Mideast I met an Arab who expressed hostility to a statement I had made about the nation Israel in a message I had given to our
tour group. Although he was a Christian Arab, he told me how he
hated the nation Israel. I said to him, "But he is your *brother*." Believe
me, that did antagonize him! He said, "I have no relationship with
him at all." I insisted that he did. I said, "You are both Semitic people.
You are a Semite as much as they are." Well, he had to admit that was
true.

So this chapter is important as it shows these relationships. The
Spirit of God uses a great deal of printer's ink to tell us about this.

We find some humor in this chapter, too.

> **These were dukes of the sons of Esau: the sons of
> Eliphaz the firstborn son of Esau; duke Teman, duke
> Omar, duke Zepho, duke Kenaz [Gen. 36:15].**

Where in the world did they get these dukes? Well, here is the beginning of nobility—they just assumed these titles. Each one of them became a duke. It is not just a nickname—they mean business by it. The
beginning of nobility is in the family of Esau.

These are the sons of Esau, who is Edom, and these are their dukes [Gen. 36:19].

They have dukes in the family now. A great many people in my country can trace their ancestry back to royalty. It makes me wonder if anybody who came from Europe were folk who worked in vineyards, made pottery, and ran shoe shops. Everybody seems to have come from royalty. Well, Esau turned out quite a few of them. In fact, he went further than producing dukes—

And these are the kings that reigned in the land of Edom, before there reigned any king over the children of Israel [Gen. 36:31].

This business of having kings was not God's plan for His people. But this was the lifestyle of Edom. They had dukes and kings over them. If you had belonged to the family of Esau, you would have needed a title, because that is the type of folk they were. It is interesting to note that the people of Esau had kings long before the people of Israel had kings. In fact, later on the people of Israel will say to Samuel, ". . . make us a king to judge us like all the nations" (1 Sam. 8:5). They could have said, "Our brothers down south, the Edomites, have kings. We would like to have kings like they do."

And these are the names of the dukes that came of Esau, according to their families, after their places, by their names; duke Timnah, duke Alvah, duke Jetheth,

Duke Aholibamah, duke Elah, duke Pinon,

Duke Kenaz, duke Teman, duke Mibzar,

Duke Magdiel, duke Iram: these be the dukes of Edom, according to their habitations in the land of their possession: he is Esau the father of the Edomites [Gen. 36:40–43].

This is the family history of the rejected line. When the chapter gives the final resumé, it lists again the dukes that came from the line of Esau. There must have been a lot of bowing and scraping to each other when they got together. "I want you to meet my brother here. He is Duke Alvah" and "I want you to meet my friend. He is Duke Timnah." And the kings—I doubt if you could even get in to see them!

This is a very interesting chapter for anyone who is interested in the study of anthropology or ethnology. A chapter like this gives a family history which probably extends farther back than any other source could go.

So the chapter closes with a list of the dukes and mentions again that their habitation is in the land of their possession which is Edom. "He is Esau the father of the Edomites." We see the working out of this in the prophecies of Obadiah and in Malachi. This is quite remarkable, friend, and something we cannot just pass by.

CHAPTER 37

THEME: Cause of strife in Jacob's family; the dreams of Joseph; Jacob sends Joseph to his brethren; Joseph sold into slavery

As we resume the story of the line of Abraham, Isaac, and Jacob, we come to the fourth outstanding fixture in this last section of Genesis. From here, all the way through the Book of Genesis, the central figure is Joseph, although we are still dealing with the family of Jacob. More chapters are devoted to Joseph than to Abraham or Isaac or to anyone else. More chapters are devoted to Joseph than to the first whole period from Genesis 1—11. This should cause the thoughtful student to pause and ask why Joseph should be given such prominence in Scripture.

There are probably several reasons. One is that the life of Joseph is a good and honorable life. He is the living example of the verse: "Finally, brethren, whatsoever things are true, whatsoever things are honest, whatsoever things are just, whatsoever things are pure, whatsoever things are lovely, whatsoever things are of good report; if there be any virtue, and if there be any praise, think on these things" (Phil. 4:8). God wants us to have whatever is good, virtuous, and great before us, and Joseph's life is just that.

There is a second reason, and it is a great one. There is no one in Scripture who is more like Christ in his person and experiences than Joseph. Yet nowhere in the New Testament is Joseph given to us as a type of Christ. However, the parallel cannot be accidental. As we go on into his story, we shall mention many of these parallels. There are at least thirty which I shall list later.

So now we resume the story of the line of Jacob which is that line leading to the Messiah, the Christ. Jacob is living in Canaan as the story of Joseph begins.

CAUSE OF STRIFE IN JACOB'S FAMILY

And Jacob dwelt in the land wherein his father was a stranger, in the land of Canaan [Gen. 37:1].

Jacob has moved down, apparently, south of Bethlehem and has come to Hebron. This is the place where Abraham had made his home. This is the place of fellowship, of communion with God.

These are the generations of Jacob. Joseph, being seventeen years old, was feeding the flock with his brethren; and the lad was with the sons of Bilhah, and with the sons of Zilpah, his father's wives: and Joseph brought unto his father their evil report [Gen. 37:2].

We can see that the bunch of boys Jacob had were real problem children (with the exception of Joseph and Benjamin). It took these men a long time to learn the lessons God would teach them.

Notice now that the emphasis shifts from Jacob to Joseph. Joseph was only seventeen, just a teenager, when this incident took place. He was the youngest of the boys out there with the flocks. Benjamin was still too young, you see, and was still at home. Joseph brought to his father a bad report about the other boys. Of course, they didn't like that. I'm sure they called him a tattletale.

Now Israel loved Joseph more than all his children, because he was the son of his old age: and he made him a coat of many colours [Gen. 37:3].

Jacob should have learned a lesson in his own home. He knew that to play favorites would cause trouble in a family. His own father had favored the elder brother, and Jacob knew what it was to be discriminated against. But here he practices the very same thing. We can understand his feelings, knowing that Rachel was the wife whom he really loved—she was the one fine thing in his life—and Joseph is really a fine boy, and Jacob loves him dearly. While all this is true, it still is not an excuse. He should not have made him that coat of many colors.

Another possible translation of "coat of many colours" would be the "coat with sleeves," a long-sleeved robe. You see, the ordinary robe in those days consisted of one piece of cloth about ten feet long. They would put a hole in the middle of it and stick the head through this hole. Half of the cloth would drop down the front of the body and half the cloth down the back of the body. They would tie it together around the waist or seam up the sides, and that would be their coat. They didn't have sleeves. So to put sleeves in the coat of any person would set him off from the others. And certainly a coat of many colors would set him apart, also.

> **And when his brethren saw that their father loved him more than all his brethren, they hated him, and could not speak peaceably unto him [Gen. 37:4].**

Naturally, the brothers hated him for being the favorite of his father. They couldn't even speak peaceably to him. So here we see strife in this family also. I tell you, I don't care whose family it is, sin will ruin it. Sin ruins lives, and sin ruins families; sin ruins communities, and it ruins nations. This is the problem with our families and cities and nations today. There is just one cause: God calls it sin.

So here we find that this boy Joseph is the object of discrimination. His father discriminates in his love for him. The brothers discriminate in their hatred against him.

THE DREAMS OF JOSEPH

> **And Joseph dreamed a dream, and he told it his brethren: and they hated him yet the more.**

> **And he said unto them, Hear, I pray you, this dream which I have dreamed [Gen. 37:5–6].**

How can we explain his conduct here? Why would he go to his father and tattle on his brothers in the first place when he knew it would incur their hatred? Well, I think he just didn't know how bad this world can be. He had no idea how bad his brothers were. I'm of the opinion that he was a rather gullible boy at this time. It took him a long time to find out about the ways of the world, but he certainly did learn. Eventually he probably knew as much about the world and the wickedness of man to man as anyone. But that was later on, not now.

You can just imagine how Joseph has been protected. His father centered all of his affection on Rachel. He had fallen in love with her at first sight and had worked fourteen years for her. Then many years went by before she bore him a child. Finally Joseph was born. What a delight that must have been for Jacob. But now Rachel is gone; so he centers his affection on this boy. He shouldn't have done that—he has other sons to raise—but that is what he has done. Joseph has been loved and protected.

> For, behold, we were binding sheaves in the field, and lo, my sheaf arose, and also stood upright; and, behold, your sheaves stood round about, and made obeisance to my sheaf.

> And his brethren said to him, Shalt thou indeed reign over us? or shalt thou indeed have dominion over us? And they hated him yet the more for his dreams, and for his words [Gen. 37:7-8].

Can't you imagine how they sneered? I'm sure they were cynical. They didn't really believe that he would rule over them. Yet, they hated him because he had this dream. This doesn't end the dreams, though. He had another one.

> And he dreamed yet another dream, and told it his brethren, and said, Behold, I have dreamed a dream more; and, behold, the sun and the moon and the eleven stars made obeisance to me.

> And he told it to his father, and to his brethren: and his father rebuked him, and said unto him, What is this

dream that thou hast dreamed? Shall I and thy mother
and thy brethren indeed come to bow down ourselves to
thee to the earth?

And his brethren envied him; but his father observed
the saying [Gen. 37:9-11].

He told them this dream and they understood what he was talking
about. This same image appears in Revelation 12:1 where a woman is
described clothed with the sun, and the moon is under her feet, and
she had a crown of twelve stars upon her head. That means the nation
of Israel. These brethren understood that Joseph was telling them
about themselves, the sons of Israel.

We are seeing the nation of Israel at its beginning here. Genesis is
like a bud, and the flower opens up as we go through the Scripture.
Here is a bud that is not going to open up until we get into the Book of
Revelation. It is a late bloomer, by the way, but it is going to open up
there. We need to understand what is being said rather than try to
make guesses. We don't need to be guessing when it is made this
clear.

Old Jacob understood it exactly, and he chided, "Does this mean
that your father, your mother, and your brothers are going to bow
down to you?" All Joseph could answer was, "That was the dream."
He didn't try to interpret it because it was evident. His brothers just
dismissed it, paid no attention to it. They thought it wasn't even in the
realm of possibility, as far as they were concerned. They knew that not
one of them would ever bow down to Joseph! But Jacob observed the
saying.

JACOB SENDS JOSEPH TO HIS BRETHREN

And his brethren went to feed their father's flock in Shechem [Gen. 37:12].

At this time, Jacob and his family were living around Hebron, which
was twenty or more miles south of Jerusalem. And Shechem is that far
north of Jerusalem, so that these boys are grazing the sheep a long

ways from home. We can see that they grazed their sheep over that entire area.

> **And Israel said unto Joseph, Do not thy brethren feed the flock in Shechem? come, and I will send thee unto them. And he said to him, Here am I [Gen. 37:13].**

Joseph said, "All right, I'll go." He was very obedient to his father, you will notice.

> **And he said to him, Go, I pray thee, see whether it be well with thy brethren, and well with the flocks; and bring me word again. So he sent him out of the vale of Hebron, and he came to Shechem [Gen. 37:14].**

Joseph had traveled all the way from Hebron to Shechem. When he reached Shechem, he began to look around for them. That is rugged terrain up there, and this boy couldn't locate them.

> **And a certain man found him, and, behold, he was wandering in the field: and the man asked him, saying, What seekest thou? [Gen. 37:15].**

I can imagine that this man had seen Joseph pass his tent several times; so he asks him who he is looking for.

> **And he said, I seek my brethren: tell me, I pray thee, where they feed their flocks.**
>
> **And the man said, They are departed hence; for I heard them say, Let us go to Dothan. And Joseph went after his brethren, and found them in Dothan [Gen. 37:16–17].**

Dothan is a long way north of Shechem. It is near the Valley of Esdraelon, and this is where the brothers have moved the sheep. And at last Joseph found them—there they were.

And when they saw him afar off, even before he came near unto them, they conspired against him to slay him.

And they said one to another, Behold, this dreamer cometh.

Come now therefore, and let us slay him, and cast him into some pit, and we will say, Some evil beast hath devoured him: and we shall see what will become of his dreams [Gen. 37:18–20].

How they hated Joseph! Here they are probably almost one hundred miles from home, and they say to each other, "Let's get rid of him now, and we'll see what will become of his dreams!"

Before we go on with the story, I want to call to your attention the comparison of Joseph to the Lord Jesus. You just should not miss the analogy.

1. The *birth* of Joseph was miraculous in that it was by the intervention of God as an answer to prayer. The Lord Jesus is virgin born. His birth was certainly miraculous!
2. Joseph was *loved* by his father. The Lord Jesus was *loved* by His Father, who declared, "This is My beloved Son."
3. Joseph had the coat of many colors which set him apart. Christ was set apart in that He was "separate from sinners."
4. Joseph announced that he was to *rule* over his brethren. The Lord Jesus presented Himself as the Messiah. Just as they ridiculed Joseph's message, so they also ridiculed Jesus. In fact, nailed to His cross were the words: THIS IS JESUS THE KING OF THE JEWS.
5. Joseph was *sent* by his father to his brethren. Jesus was *sent* to His brethren—He came first to the lost sheep of the house of Israel.
6. Joseph was *hated* by his brethren without a cause, and the Lord Jesus was *hated* by His brethren without a cause.

As we return to the story now, remember that Joseph is approaching his brothers, and they are plotting against him. He is wearing that coat of many colors or with the sleeves, which was a mark of position.

We must remember that Joseph was younger than his brothers yet was in a position above them. So there is all this hatred and jealousy—to the point of murder!

Reuben has already lost his position as the firstborn. However, he stands in a good light here. He has more mature judgment than the others.

> **And Reuben heard it, and he delivered him out of their hands; and said, Let us not kill him [Gen. 37:21].**

They would have killed him right then and there if Reuben had not intervened.

> **And Reuben said unto them, Shed no blood, but cast him into this pit that is in the wilderness, and lay no hand upon him; that he might rid him out of their hands, to deliver him to his father again [Gen. 37:22].**

It was Reuben's avowed purpose, after Joseph had been put into the pit, to slip back again and take him out of the pit and take him home to his father.

> **And it came to pass, when Joseph was come unto his brethren, that they stripped Joseph out of his coat, his coat of many colours that was on him [Gen. 37:23].**

That coat Joseph wore was like waving a red flag in front of a bull. They hated it because it set him apart from them. According to the law of primogeniture, the older brothers had a prior claim; so they stripped off from Joseph the hated coat.

> **And they took him, and cast him into a pit: and the pit was empty, there was no water in it.**
>
> **And they sat down to eat bread: and they lifted up their eyes and looked, and behold, a company of Ishmeelites**

> came from Gilead with their camels bearing spicery
> and balm and myrrh, going to carry it down to Egypt
> [Gen. 37:24-25].

This was a caravan of traders that was going by.

> And Judah said unto his brethren, What profit is it if we
> slay our brother, and conceal his blood?
>
> Come, and let us sell him to the Ishmeelites, and let not
> our hand be upon him; for he is our brother and our
> flesh. And his brethren were content [Gen. 37:26-27].

Now Judah intervenes when he sees some traders going by. It is a very
mercenary plan that he has, but at least he doesn't want murder to
take place. He doesn't want the blood of Joseph to be on their hands.
The brothers were satisfied with the suggestion because what they
wanted was to get rid of him—they didn't care how it was accomplished. They realized the Ishmeelites would take him down to Egypt
and would sell him there as a slave. At least they would be rid of him.
Slavery in most places was a living death, and they knew they would
certainly never hear from him again.

> Then there passed by Midianites merchantmen; and
> they drew and lifted up Joseph out of the pit, and sold
> Joseph to the Ishmeelites for twenty pieces of silver: and
> they brought Joseph to Egypt [Gen. 37:28].

At this point you are probably thinking that Moses (who wrote the
Genesis record) should make up his mind. First he calls them
Ishmeelites, then Midianites, and then he calls them Ishmeelites
again. So who are they? Is this an error in the Bible? Some time ago a
student brought to me a little booklet, which had been handed to him,
listing a thousand or two thousand so-called errors in the Bible. After
looking it over, the only errors I found were in that little book—not in
the Bible. One of the so-called errors was this matter of calling the

men of this caravan Ishmeelites, then Midianites, then Ishmeelites again.

This is an interesting point, and it deserves a closer look. First of all, it reveals how the critic and those who hate the Bible can interpret as an error something that actually shows the accuracy of the biblical record.

Who are the Ishmeelites? They are the descendants of Ishmael, the son of Abraham. Who are the Midianites? They are the descendants of Midian, a son of Abraham. Ishmael was the son of Abraham by Hagar, and Midian was the son of Abraham by Keturah whom he married after the death of Sarah. They are all brethren—they are actually kin to this group of boys who are selling their brother! At this time, who was an Israelite? Well, there were only twelve of them. How many Ishmeelites do you think there might be by this time? Ishmael was older than Isaac, so maybe there were one hundred or more. How many Midianites would there be? Well, Midian was born after Isaac; so there couldn't be too many—maybe a dozen or more. These were little groups, and in that day travel was dangerous. They were going across the desert to Egypt. They joined together for protection, and they joined together for a common interest. They were going on a business trip to Egypt, and, since they were related, they understood each other and joined together.

May I say that the Word of God makes good sense if you just let it make good sense. We are the folk that don't make the good sense. Ignorance adds a great deal to what people consider contradictions in the Bible. You can see that Moses understood what the situation was, and he wrote precisely.

JOSEPH SOLD INTO SLAVERY

So the brothers sell Joseph to the Ishmaelites who take him down to Egypt.

And Reuben returned unto the pit; and, behold, Joseph was not in the pit; and he rent his clothes.

> And he returned unto his brethren, and said, The child
> is not; and I, whither shall I go?
>
> And they took Joseph's coat, and killed a kid of the
> goats, and dipped the coat in the blood [Gen. 37:29–31].

Scripture does not tell us whether they told Reuben what they actually
had done, but I'm of the opinion they did. And they probably said it
was no use chasing after the merchants because they were a long way
off by now; so he might as well help them think up a good story to tell
Jacob.

> And they sent the coat of many colours, and they
> brought it to their father; and said, This have we found:
> know now whether it be thy son's coat or no [Gen.
> 37:32].

Pretty clever, isn't it? They act as if they had never seen Joseph. They
pretend they just found this coat. Believe me, they knew that hated
coat! But they pretend they don't recognize it and ask their father
whether he recognizes it. Jacob knew whose coat it was. He comes to a
natural conclusion and, of course, the conclusion to which the brothers intended for him to come.

> And he knew it, and said, It is my son's coat; an evil
> beast hath devoured him; Joseph is without doubt rent
> in pieces [Gen. 37:33].

Let's pause and take another look at this. They killed a kid of the goats
and used that blood on the coat. Does this matter of deceiving a father
with a goat remind us of something we've heard before? Remember
that when Rebekah and Jacob were conniving, they used a kid for the
savory meat dish, and they took the skin of the goat and put it on the
hands and arms of Jacob to deceive his father. Now the brothers of
Joseph are using the blood of a goat to deceive their father, who is none

other than Jacob himself. They hand the coat to him and say, "Do you recognize it? We just found it up there in the mountains. It looks like a wild beast must have got to him." Old Jacob came to the conclusion that his son Joseph had been killed.

Notice this very carefully. Jacob is deceived in exactly the same way that he had deceived. "Be not deceived; God is not mocked: for whatsoever a man soweth, that shall he also reap" (Gal. 6:7)—not something else, not something similar, but the *same thing*. This man Jacob did some bad sowing. He used deception, and now that he is a father, he is deceived in the identical way that he had deceived his own father years before.

When we sow corn, we reap corn. When we sow tares, we reap tares. We get exactly what we sow. This is true in any realm you wish to move in today. It is true in the physical realm, in the moral, and in the spiritual realm. That is true also for the believer. If you think you can get by with sin because you are a child of God, you have another thought coming. In fact, you'd better take that other thought and not commit the sin because God is no respecter of persons. He said this is the way it is going to be, and you are not an exception. I talked to a minister who had gotten involved with another man's wife. As I talked with him, he tried to justify himself on the basis that he was someone special to the Lord. He felt that because he was who he was, he could operate on a little different plane and by a different rule book than anyone else. But he found that God is no respecter of persons.

Now notice the grief of Jacob—

> **And Jacob rent his clothes, and put sackcloth upon his loins, and mourned for his son many days.**
>
> **And all his sons and all his daughters rose up to comfort him; but he refused to be comforted: and he said, For I will go down into the grave unto my son mourning. Thus his father wept for him [Gen. 37:34–35].**

Perhaps some will think his grief is a demonstration of how much Jacob loved his son Joseph. I'll admit that he certainly loved this boy.

But it reveals that Jacob had not learned to walk by faith yet, friend. You recall the experience he had at Peniel. It was the deflation of the old ego. The flesh collapsed there, but now he must learn to walk by faith. He hasn't learned that yet. In fact, the faith of Jacob is mentioned in the eleventh chapter of Hebrews, but nothing in his life is mentioned there as an example of his faith until the time of his death. Then faith is exhibited.

Compare his grief here to the grief of a man like David (2 Sam. 12:15–23). David wept over the baby boy of his who died. He loved that little one just as much as Jacob loved Joseph, but David was a man of faith. He knew the little one couldn't come back to him, and he also knew that he was going to the little fellow some day. What faith! You see, Jacob is not walking by faith, friend. This is abnormal grief.

Christian friend, perhaps you have lost a loved one. Perhaps you just can't get over it. I want to say to you kindly, not brutally, but kindly: learn to walk by faith. You manifest faith when you recognize that you can't bring that one back by grieving. It does no good at all. If you are a child of God and you are grieving over one who is a child of God, then walk by faith. You will see that one again and never be separated. The world has no faith—they grieve as those without hope. Christian friend, you can walk by faith.

Now the final verse of this chapter follows Joseph to Egypt—

And the Midianites sold him into Egypt unto Potiphar, an officer of Pharaoh's, and captain of the guard [Gen. 37:36].

We will leave Joseph right there and pick up his story in chapter 39.

CHAPTER 38

This is another chapter that seems to be about as necessary as a fifth leg on a cow. After you have read the story, you may wish that it had been left out of the Bible. Many people have asked me why this chapter is in the Word of God. I agree that it is one of the worst chapters in the Bible, but it gives us some background on the tribe of Judah, out of which the Lord Jesus Christ came. This fact makes it important that it be included in the biblical record. In this chapter you will read names like Judah and Tamar and Pharez and Zerah. If you think they sound familiar, it is because you have read them in the first chapter of Matthew. They are in the genealogy of the Lord Jesus Christ. My friend, that is an amazing thing! Our Lord came into a sinful line. He was made in all points like as we are, yet He Himself was without sin. He came into that human line where all have sinned and come short of the glory of God.

This chapter deals with the sin and the shame of Judah. This leads me to say that the sons of Jacob were certainly not very much of a comfort to him. It looks as if all the sons were problem children, with the exception of Joseph and Benjamin. And Joseph was no comfort because his father was heartbroken about his disappearance. All of this reveals to us that Jacob spent too much time in Padan-aram accumulating a fortune rather than teaching his children. How different he was from Abraham. You remember that God had said of Abraham: "For I know him, that he will command his children and his household after him, and they shall keep the way of the LORD, to do justice and judgment; that the LORD may bring upon Abraham that which he hath spoken of him" (Gen. 18:19).

Well, Jacob didn't do that. He was so busy down there contending with Uncle Laban that he didn't have much time for his boys. That was tragic, because each one of them seemed to have gotten involved in something that was very sinful.

There is, I believe, a further reason for including this chapter in the Word of God at this juncture. Beginning with the next chapter, we go down to the land of Egypt with Joseph. God is sending Joseph ahead, as he very clearly detected from the fortuitous concurrence of circumstances in his life, to prepare the way for the coming down of the children of Israel into Egypt. It would preserve their lives during the famine in Canaan, but more than that, it would get them out of the land of Canaan from the abominable Canaanites into the seclusion of the land of Goshen in Egypt. Had Jacob and his family continued on in Canaan, they would have dropped down to the level of the Canaanites. The chapter before us reveals the necessity of getting the family of Jacob away from the degrading influence of the Canaanites.

This is the story of Judah, whose line will be the kingly line among the tribes of Israel.

> **And it came to pass at that time, that Judah went down from his brethren, and turned in to a certain Adullamite, whose name was Hirah.**

> **And Judah saw there a daughter of a certain Canaanite, whose name was Shuah; and he took her, and went in unto her [Gen. 38:1–2].**

He went down to do business with a certain Adullamite, and when he got down there he saw this Canaanite woman, and he had an affair with her.

> **And she conceived, and bare a son; and he called his name Er [Gen. 38:3].**

Judah called his name Er—and Judah certainly had *erred*; he had sinned.

> **And she conceived again, and bare a son; and she called his name Onan.**

> **And she yet again conceived, and bare a son; and called**

his name Shelah: and he was at Chezib, when she bare him.

And Judah took a wife for Er his firstborn, whose name was Tamar [Gen. 38:4–6].

This is the first appearance of Tamar. She gets into the genealogy of Christ this way! Now, look at this family. It is just loaded with sin.

And Er, Judah's firstborn, was wicked in the sight of the LORD; and the LORD slew him.

And Judah said unto Onan, Go in unto thy brother's wife, and marry her, and raise up seed to thy brother.

And Onan knew that the seed should not be his; and it came to pass, when he went in unto his brother's wife, that he spilled it on the ground, lest that he should give seed to his brother.

And the thing which he did displeased the LORD: wherefore he slew him also [Gen. 38:7–10].

This reminds us of the present hour when there is so much emphasis on sex.

Then said Judah to Tamar his daughter in law, Remain a widow at thy father's house, till Shelah my son be grown: for he said, Lest peradventure he die also, as his brethren did. And Tamar went and dwelt in her father's house [Gen. 38:11].

It was the custom of that day that when a man died, his brother was to marry his widow. Onan refused to do it, and he was smitten with death.

Now Judah has another son who is growing up, and he tells his daughter-in-law to follow the custom of returning to her father's house until the younger son is ready for marriage.

> And in process of time the daughter of Shuah Judah's
> wife died; and Judah was comforted, and went up unto
> his sheepshearers to Timnath, he and his friend Hirah
> the Adullamite.
>
> And it was told Tamar, saying, Behold thy father in law
> goeth up to Timnath to shear his sheep [Gen. 38:12–13].

Apparently this deal that Judah had, which concerned seeing this
Adullamite by the name of Hirah, was in connection with sheep. They
were raising sheep and must have had a tremendous flock together.
Judah goes up there to shear them. In the meantime, Tamar has been
waiting all this while at home. She comes to the conclusion that Judah
is not going to give Shelah to her as her husband.

> And she put her widow's garments off from her, and cov-
> ered her with a veil, and wrapped herself, and sat in an
> open place, which is by the way to Timnath; for she saw
> that Shelah was grown, and she was not given unto him
> to wife [Gen. 38:14].

Shelah was, of course, the third son of Judah. Tamar sees that Judah
doesn't intend to give her to him as his wife; so she takes action. She
takes off her widow's clothes and sits by the wayside with her face
covered as was the custom of harlots.

> And he turned unto her by the way, and said, Go to, I
> pray thee, let me come in unto thee; (for he knew not
> that she was his daughter in law.) And she said, What
> wilt thou give me, that thou mayest come in unto me?
> [Gen. 38:16].

We get a picture of Judah. He had propositioned the Canaanite
woman, Shuah's daughter. Now he does the same thing with Tamar.
This is a very black picture and an ugly story that we have here. Judah

thought she was a harlot. She saw the opportunity of taking advantage of him, and she did it.

> And he said, I will send thee a kid from the flock. And she said, Wilt thou give me a pledge, till thou send it?

> And he said, What pledge shall I give thee? And she said, Thy signet, and thy bracelets, and thy staff that is in thine hand. And he gave it her, and came in unto her, and she conceived by him.

> And she arose, and went away, and laid by her veil from her, and put on the garments of her widowhood.

> And Judah sent the kid by the hand of his friend the Adullamite, to receive his pledge from the woman's hand; but he found her not [Gen. 38:17–20].

Judah sent his friend into town who said, "I'm looking for the harlot that is here."

> Then he asked the men of that place, saying, Where is the harlot, that was openly by the way side? And they said, There was no harlot in this place.

> And he returned to Judah, and said, I cannot find her; and also the men of the place said, that there was no harlot in this place.

> And Judah said, Let her take it to her, lest we be shamed: behold, I sent this kid, and thou hast not found her.

> And it came to pass about three months after, that it was told Judah, saying, Tamar thy daughter in law hath played the harlot; and also, behold, she is with child by whoredom. And Judah said, Bring her forth, and let her be burnt [Gen. 38:21–24].

That's Judah. Here is the old double standard. God doesn't approve of these things, friend. It is here in His Word, but that doesn't mean that He approves of it. His people are acting just like the Canaanites, which is the reason He is going to get them out of this land and take them down into the land of Egypt. There He is going to separate them and isolate them in the land of Goshen to get them away from this terrible influence. This episode reveals the necessity for God to do this.

Judah is acting in a way that is unspeakable it is so bad. The fact of the matter is, he is quick to see the sin in somebody else, but he can't see it in himself. It reminds us of the time Nathan went in to David and told him the story about the fellow who had one little ewe lamb. When Nathan said the rich man came and took it away, David was quick to condemn the rich man. David reacted just like Judah does here. David said he wanted the rich man stoned to death. Then Nathan declared that David himself was the man. It is interesting that we can all see sin so clearly in other people, but we can't see it within our own being.

The charge against Judah is really a double one. His sin is terrible in itself, but it was with his own daughter-in-law! This is the way the Canaanites lived. We think that we are in a sex revolution today and there is a *new* sexual freedom. My friend, for centuries the heathen have had sexual freedom. That's part of heathendom, and it is the reason they lived as low as they did. It is the reason they were judged and removed from the scene. The Canaanites are gone. They have disappeared. God has judged them. That ought to be a message to any person. Yet a great many people don't seem to get the message—even Christians! You wonder why this chapter is in the Bible. It is in the Bible as a warning to us. It is in the Bible to let us know that God did not approve of sin, and it explains why God took Israel out of the land of Palestine and down into the land of Egypt.

Tamar is then brought into the presence of her father-in-law.

When she was brought forth, she sent to her father in law, saying, By the man, whose these are, am I with child: and she said, Discern, I pray thee, whose are these, the signet, and bracelets, and staff [Gen. 38:25].

Judah was going to have her burnt. But she said, "Well, I would like you to know who the father of the child is; he is the one who owns these articles that I'm showing you." Judah looked at them and had to admit they were his own.

> **And Judah acknowledged them, and said, She hath been more righteous than I; because that I gave her not to Shelah my son. And he knew her again no more [Gen. 38:26].**

This was repulsive even to Judah, but we can see how he had adopted some of the customs of the Canaanites.

May I pause for a moment to make an application? Remember, all these things are written for our learning. They are examples unto us. Today we hear that if we are going to witness to this generation and if we are going to communicate to them, we've got to get down to their level. I disagree with that. God has never used that method to witness. God has always, under all circumstances, asked His people to live on a high and lofty plane.

I can well imagine one of our present-day theologians going up to Noah and saying, "Brother Noah, you're spending all your time working on this boat, and it is silly for you to be doing that. We're having a big party over in Babylon tonight. They just got a new shipment of marijuana and we are really going to blow our minds. We're going to pass around the grass and we're going to have a high time and take a little trip. You don't need to build that boat for a trip; we'll give you a trip. Come on over." Noah, of course, would refuse. So the theologian would ask Noah, "How do you expect to reach all the hippies of Babylon? How are you going to reach the Babylonian beboppers unless you are willing to come down and communicate with them?" The fact of the matter is, God never asked Noah to come down to "communicate." God asked him to give *His* message.

And this is what God asks us to do in our day. I am firmly convinced that if God's people would give out His Word and live lives that would commend the gospel, He would make their witness effective. There are many pastors in our day who are so afraid they will lose the crowd that they do anything to attract people to their church—and some of them are having their problems. But God has never asked us to compromise. God does ask us to give out the Word of God—regardless of the size of our congregation.

This reminds me of the story about Dr. Scofield who was invited to speak over in North Carolina. The first service was on a rainy night, and very few people came to hear him speak. The pastor felt that he must apologize to Dr. Scofield; so he reached over and told him that he was sorry so few people had come to hear a man of his caliber. Dr. Scofield replied to the pastor, "My Lord had only twelve men to speak to, and since He had only twelve men and never complained, who is C. I. Scofield that he should complain about a small crowd?" Friend, this is a lesson for our generation to learn. We so often think that there must be crowds or else God is not in it. Maybe God has called us to witness to a few. But I have news for you: If you give out the Word of God, it will have its effect. My friend, the Word of God is powerful, and God is looking for clean vessels through whom he can give it out.

Well, Judah had certainly lowered himself to the level of the Canaanites, and look at the results.

> And it came to pass in the time of her travail, that, behold, twins were in her womb.
>
> And it came to pass, when she travailed, that the one put out his hand: and the midwife took and bound upon his hand a scarlet thread, saying, This came out first.
>
> And it came to pass, as he drew back his hand, that, behold, his brother came out: and she said, How hast thou broken forth? this breach be upon thee: therefore his name was called Pharez.
>
> And afterward came out his brother, that had the scarlet thread upon his hand: and his name was called Zerah [Gen. 38:27–30].

Now if we turn over to the New Testament, we will find the genealogy of the Lord Jesus in Matthew, chapter 1. There we read: "Abraham begat Isaac; and Isaac begat Jacob; and Jacob begat Judas and his brethren; and Judas begat Phares and Zara of Thamar; and Phares begat Esrom; and Esrom begat Aram" (Matt. 1:2–3). Then as we follow through the genealogy, we come to this verse: "And Jacob begat Joseph the husband of Mary, of whom was born Jesus, who is called Christ" (Matt. 1:16). It is an amazing thing that the Lord Jesus Christ, according to the flesh, should come through the line of Judah and Tamar! When He came into the human family, He came in a sinful line. He was made sin for us, He who knew no sin, that we might be made the righteousness of God in Him (see 2 Cor. 5:21).

CHAPTER 39

THEME: Overseer in the house of Potiphar; tempted, then framed by Potiphar's wife; Joseph imprisoned

We return to the story of Joseph after the interlude of chapter 38, which we classified as one of the worst chapters in the Bible because it certainly tells a sordid story of the man Judah.

We will discover that Joseph is altogether different from Judah. I have always felt that Joseph and Benjamin got a great deal of teaching, instruction, and personal attention that the other ten boys did not receive. These seemed to be the only two boys in whom Jacob was interested.

Because of the hatred and animosity of Joseph's brothers, he was sold into slavery and taken to the land of Egypt.

To be in a foreign land and sold into slavery is a very dreary prospect for a seventeen-year-old boy. There is certainly nothing in the outward aspect of things to bring any encouragement to his heart. Joseph seems to be more or less a hardluck boy. Even in the land of Egypt, just as things would begin to move smoothly for him, something else would happen. Of course, it always happened for a purpose, even though that was difficult for Joseph to see.

There is no person in the Old Testament in whose life the purpose of God is more clearly seen than Joseph. The providence of God is manifest in every detail of his life. The hand of God is upon him and the leading of the Lord is evident, but Joseph is the one patriarch to whom God did not appear directly, according to the text of Scripture. God appeared to Abraham, Isaac, and Jacob, but not to Joseph. Yet the direction of God in his life is more clearly seen than in any other. He is the Old Testament example of Romans 8:28: "And we know that all things work together for good to them that love God, to them who are the called according to his purpose." Joseph himself expressed it in rather vivid language. At the death of their father, Joseph's brothers felt that Joseph might turn on them, and they came to him asking for mercy. He told them that he held no grudge against them at all and said, "But as for you, ye thought evil against me; but God meant it unto good, to bring to pass, as it is this day, to save much people alive" (Gen. 50:20). Although everything seemed to go wrong for him and the outward aspect was dark—it looked *terrible*—each event was a step bringing to fruition God's purpose in this man's life.

My friend, in our own lives we need to reckon on the fact that ". . . whom the Lord loveth he chasteneth, and scourgeth every son whom he receiveth" (Heb. 12:6). If we are the children of God, in the will of God, we can have the assurance of God that nothing comes to us without His permission. God works all things together for good to them who love Him. Even our misfortunes, heartbreaks, and sufferings are for our good and His glory.

There is a hedge about every child of God, and nothing gets through it without the permission of God. You remember that, when Satan wanted to test Job, he said to God: "Hast not thou made an hedge about him, and about his house, and about all that he hath on every side? thou hast blessed the work of his hands, and his substance is increased in the land" (Job 1:10). Satan asked God to let the hedge down. Even if Satan gets God's permission to test us, still all things will work for our good.

Dr. Torrey used to say that Romans 8:28 is the soft pillow for a tired heart. And someone else has put it like this: "God nothing does, nor suffers to be done, but what we would ourselves, if we but could see through all events of things as well as He."

There is another aspect of the life of Joseph which should be an encouragement to every child of God. None of God's children today have ever had a direct revelation from God. Some modern false prophets claim to the contrary, but God has not appeared directly to any person today. It is for our encouragement that God did not appear to Joseph directly because we can still know that He is leading and directing us.

Now let's follow this young man Joseph and see what is going to happen to him.

OVERSEER IN THE HOUSE OF POTIPHAR

And Joseph was brought down to Egypt; and Potiphar, an officer of Pharaoh, captain of the guard, an Egyptian bought him of the hands of the Ishmeelites, which had brought him down thither [Gen. 39:1].

This fine-looking young man, seventeen years old, would be a prize as a slave in the market. He was bought by Potiphar who was a captain of the guard. Potiphar was in the military, he had his office in the Pentagon of that day, and he was part of the brass, a prominent official.

And the LORD was with Joseph, and he was a prosperous man; and he was in the house of his master the Egyptian [Gen. 39:2].

Immediately, when he gets into the home of Potiphar who is an officer of Pharaoh, it is obvious that the Lord is with Joseph. Blessing came to that home when Joseph came.

And his master saw that the LORD was with him, and that the LORD made all that he did to prosper in his hand [Gen. 39:3].

Life is great up to this point. You'd like to add that they all lived happily ever after, but they didn't. This is not a story; it is reality. The child of God is going to encounter temptation, trouble, and problems in this world. This is what is going to happen to Joseph.

And Joseph found grace in his sight, and he served him: and he made him overseer over his house, and all that he had he put into his hand [Gen. 39:4].

Just think of this! Because of the way Joseph serves, he is elevated to the position of handling all the material substance—the chattels and probably even the real estate—of Potiphar. The man trusted him with everything.

> **And it came to pass from the time that he had made him overseer in his house, and over all that he had, that the LORD blessed the Egyptian's house for Joseph's sake; and the blessing of the LORD was upon all that he had in the house, and in the field.**
>
> **And he left all that he had in Joseph's hand; and he knew not aught he had, save the bread which he did eat. And Joseph was a goodly person, and well favoured [Gen. 39:5–6].**

Potiphar trusted Joseph so much that he never even demanded an accounting—he didn't have to hire a C.P.A. to go over the books. He believed in the integrity of this young man. The only thing that Potiphar worried about, as an officer of Pharaoh, was that he should please Pharaoh and do a good job there. He let Joseph handle his personal affairs. When he sat down at the table, the food was put before him. That's all that he was interested in because he trusted this young man.

TEMPTED, THEN FRAMED BY POTIPHAR'S WIFE

Now notice what happens—

> **And it came to pass after these things, that his master's wife cast her eyes upon Joseph; and she said, Lie with me [Gen. 39:7].**

Potiphar had given him the full run of his home, and Joseph had charge of everything. While Joseph was busy, Potiphar's wife was also busy. She was busy scheming. Joseph was a handsome young man. It may be that Potiphar was an old man because it was generally the custom in that day for an older man to have a young wife. She sees Joseph, and she attempts to entice him.

But he refused, and said unto his master's wife, Behold,
my master wotteth not what is with me in the house, and
he hath committed all that he hath to my hand;

There is none greater in this house than I; neither hath
he kept back any thing from me but thee, because thou
art his wife: how then can I do this great wickedness,
and sin against God? [Gen. 39:8-9].

Now do you notice that this young man is serving God in all of this?
When he went down to Egypt, it was a land filled with idolatry just as
much as Babylon was. In that land of idolatry, Joseph maintained a
testimony for the living and true God and a high moral standard.
When this woman enticed him, he said, "My master has turned over
everything to me but you—you are his *wife.*" Notice what a high viewpoint Joseph had on marriage.

You see, God has given marriage to all mankind. When a person
begins to despise the marriage vows, he is beginning to despise God,
my friend. A man who will break his marriage vows will generally
break any vow he has made to God. It has been interesting for me to
note in my ministry that a divorced person, that is, one who gets divorced because he or she has been unfaithful, generally will get as far
from God as any person possibly can. I've seen that happen again and
again.

Joseph here is attempting to be true to God. What a high viewpoint
he has! Yet, look at what is going to come to pass because he attempts
to serve the living and true God.

And it came to pass, as she spake to Joseph day by day,
that he hearkened not unto her, to lie by her, or to be with
her [Gen. 39:10].

This man, Potiphar, as an officer of Pharaoh, would be away from
home a great deal. Maybe he was away from home too much. This
woman didn't tempt Joseph only one time, but again and again and
again. It was a constant temptation to him, yet this young man did not

yield. You can imagine that there begins to well up in her a boiling resentment against Joseph. The old bromide has it, "Hell hath no fury like that of a woman scorned." Believe me, she is going to take revenge on Joseph.

> **And it came to pass about this time, that Joseph went into the house to do his business; and there was none of the men of the house there within.**
>
> **And she caught him by his garment, saying, Lie with me: and he left his garment in her hand, and fled, and got him out.**
>
> **And it came to pass, when she saw that he had left his garment in her hand, and was fled forth,**
>
> **That she called unto the men of her house, and spake unto them, saying, See, he hath brought in an Hebrew unto us to mock us; he came in unto me to lie with me, and I cried with a loud voice [Gen. 39:11–14].**

Things weren't so well between Potiphar and his wife. Notice how she speaks of him in such a mean, degrading way. She says that *he* brought in a Hebrew to mock them. In other words, the wife probably had been guilty of this before. The man whom I feel most sorry for is Potiphar. He is the sap if there ever was one. Possibly he suspected something all along.

She is beginning now to cover up her tracks—

> **And it came to pass, when he heard that I lifted up my voice, and cried, that he left his garment with me, and fled, and got him out.**
>
> **And she laid up his garment by her, until his lord came home [Gen. 39:15–16].**

So here is the boy Joseph in his teens, down there alone in Egypt, and he is being framed in the most dastardly manner. She brings this charge against Joseph to the other men. Her husband was away from home; so she has all this story built up to tell him when he arrives.

> And she spake unto him, according to these words, saying, The Hebrew servant, which thou hast brought unto us, came in unto me to mock:
>
> And it came to pass, as I lifted up my voice and cried, that he left his garment with me, and fled out.
>
> And it came to pass, when his master heard the words of his wife, which she spake unto him, saying, After this manner did thy servant to me; that his wrath was kindled [Gen. 39:17–19].

On the surface it seems that Potiphar believes her story, at least it made him angry at the moment. He was an officer in the army of Pharaoh and must have been a pretty sharp man to be among the brass. But he certainly was a stupid husband. It is my personal feeling that he recognized the kind of wife he had and thought the expedient thing was to throw Joseph into prison and forget the whole matter. I feel sorry for him, married to this woman. I'm of the opinion that she had been unfaithful many times before and that Joseph was just another one in her series of conquests—only it just didn't work with Joseph, so she framed him.

JOSEPH IMPRISONED

> And Joseph's master took him, and put him into the prison, a place where the king's prisoners were bound: and he was there in the prison [Gen. 39:20].

This boy is certainly having bad luck, is he not? There at home he was the favorite of his father, wearing a coat of many colors. The next thing he knew, his brothers had taken off the coat and put him down in a pit. He hears them dickering with some tradesmen, and then he is sold down to Egypt. He was only seventeen years old, and I am of the opinion that on the way down, and after he got there, he spent many nights wetting the pillow with his tears. He certainly was homesick.

Now he's getting along in this new position, just elevated to a high position because he is a capable and fine-looking young man. Then the wife of Potiphar attempts to lure him to commit sin. His high moral standard prevents him from yielding. As a result of that, she frames him. This poor boy just doesn't stand a chance.

We need to remember that, although Joseph had been elevated in his position, he is still a slave. Potiphar's wife would be like Caesar's wife—one just wouldn't dare say anything about her. Obviously her word would be accepted. Poor Joseph! He doesn't need to even open his mouth. He is declared guilty before he can make any kind of a defense at all. He immediately finds himself put into prison, the prison where the prisoners of Pharaoh were placed.

> **But the LORD was with Joseph, and shewed him mercy, and gave him favour in the sight of the keeper of the prison.**
>
> **And the keeper of the prison committed to Joseph's hand all the prisoners that were in the prison; and whatsoever they did there, he was the doer of it.**
>
> **The keeper of the prison looked not to any thing that was under his hand; because the LORD was with him, and that which he did, the LORD made it to prosper [Gen. 39:21–23].**

The hand of God is obvious in this young man's life, but over against it are the terrible things that happen to him. Now he finds himself in prison. How discouraging that would have been to the average person. But the interesting thing is that the Lord is with Joseph. Although He does not appear to him, as He had to the other patriarchs, He shows him mercy. First He causes the keeper of the prison to like him and to trust him. Although Joseph is naturally a very attractive young man and has tremendous ability, the important thing to note is that all of this would have come to naught had not God been with him. God is with him and is leading him. All of these experiences are moving toward the accomplishment of a purpose in this young man's life.

Joseph recognized this, and it gave him a buoyancy, an attitude of optimism. The circumstances did not get him down. He lived on top of his circumstances. I have a preacher friend who tells me my problem is that the circumstances are all on top of me! I think many of us live that way. But Joseph was one who was living on top of his circumstances. The Lord was with him. He recognized the hand of God in his life, and so he was not discouraged. Discouragement is one of the finest weapons Satan has—discouragement and disappointment. This young man seems to have surmounted all of his circumstances. He reminds us of the passage in Hebrews: "Now no chastening for the present seemeth to be joyous, but grievous: nevertheless afterward it yieldeth the peaceable fruit of righteousness unto them which are exercised thereby" (Heb. 12:11).

Certainly the chastening of the Lord is going to yield the peaceable fruit of righteousness in the life of this young man.

The story of Joseph reveals that not every man has his price. Satan says that he does, but there have been several men whom Satan could not buy. Joseph was one of these. Job was another, and the apostle Paul was still another. Satan despises mankind, but these and many more are men whom Satan found he could not buy.

Is it the will of God that Joseph be in prison? Well, my friend, it is almost essential that he be there. We'll see that in the next chapter.

CHAPTER 40

THEME: Joseph interprets dreams for the butler and baker; fulfillment of the dreams

This chapter, rather than advancing the story of Joseph, seems to slow it down to absolutely no movement at all. We see Joseph in prison, and he is delayed and circumscribed by the ingratitude of the chief butler of Pharaoh. We may ask what all this means. May I say to you that all of this is accomplishing God's plan and purpose in Joseph's life. We will see this as we get into the chapter.

In chapter 37 we started a comparison between Joseph and the Lord Jesus. Now that we are farther along in the story, let us stop to make some more comparisons:

1. Joseph was sent to his brethren. The Lord Jesus Christ was sent to His brethren, the lost sheep of the house of Israel.
2. Joseph was hated by his brethren without a cause, and this is what the Lord Jesus says about Himself, "They hated me without a cause."
3. Joseph was sold by his own brothers, and the Lord Jesus was sold by one of His own brethren.
4. Joseph was sold for twenty pieces of silver. The Lord Jesus was sold for thirty pieces of silver.
5. The brothers plotted to kill Joseph. The brethren plotted to kill the Lord Jesus—"He came unto His own, and His own received Him not."
6. Joseph was put into the pit which was meant to be a place of death for him. The Lord Jesus was crucified.
7. Joseph was raised up out of that pit. The Lord Jesus was raised from the dead on the third day.
8. Joseph obeyed his father. The Lord Jesus obeyed His Father so that He could say that He always did the things which pleased His Father.
9. Joseph's father had sent him to seek his brethren. We are told

that the Lord Jesus Christ came to do the will of His Father when he came here not seek His brethren.

10. Joseph was mocked by his brethren. When they saw him coming, they said, "Behold, this dreamer cometh." The Lord Jesus was mocked by His brethren. When He was on the Cross, they said, "If He be the Christ, let Him come down now from the cross."

11. The brothers refused to receive Joseph, and the brethren of the Lord Jesus, the Jews, refused to receive Him.

12. They took counsel to kill Joseph, and we are told they took counsel to plot the death of the Lord Jesus.

13. Joseph's coat dripping with blood was returned to his father. They took the coat of the Lord Jesus and gambled for it.

14. After Joseph was sold into Egypt, he was lost sight of for many years. Christ ascended up into heaven. He told His disciples that they should see Him no more until His return.

15. Joseph was tempted by the world, the flesh, and the Devil, and he resisted. The Lord Jesus was tempted by the world, the flesh, and the Devil, and He won the victory.

16. Joseph became the savior of the world during this period, in the physical sense—he saved them from starvation. The Lord Jesus Christ in every sense is the Savior of the whole world.

17. Joseph was hated by his brothers, and they delivered him to the Gentiles. He couldn't defend himself, and he was unjustly accused. The Lord Jesus was also delivered by His own to the religious rulers who in turn delivered Him to the Gentiles. He was innocent.

18. Pilate did not believe the accusation which was brought against the Lord Jesus. He found Him innocent, yet he scourged Him. And Joseph had to suffer although Potiphar probably knew that he was innocent. Potiphar had to keep up a front before Pharaoh as Pilate had to keep up a front before Caesar.

19. Joseph found favor in the sight of the jailer. And in the case of Jesus, the Roman centurion said of Him, "Truly, this was the Son of God."

20. Joseph was numbered with the transgressors. He was a blessing to the butler, and he was judgment for the baker. The Lord Jesus was crucified between two thieves. One was judged and the other was blessed.

In the chapter before us we will begin to see why it was the will of God that Joseph be in prison at this time.

JOSEPH INTERPRETS DREAMS FOR THE BUTLER AND BAKER

And it came to pass after these things, that the butler of the king of Egypt and his baker had offended their lord the king of Egypt.·

And Pharaoh was wroth against two of his officers, against the chief of the butlers, and against the chief of the bakers.

And he put them in ward in the house of the captain of the guard, into the prison, the place where Joseph was bound [Gen. 40:1–3].

That was no accident!

What does this reveal? It certainly reveals to us the arbitrary and dictatorial position and policy that the pharaohs of Egypt had. I don't know what the baker did—maybe he burned the biscuits for breakfast. For some whim, Pharaoh put him into prison. What did the butler do? Maybe he was bringing up a glass of wine to Pharaoh and stubbed his toe and spilled it on the Persian rug that was there. I don't know. It isn't told us why both the baker and the butler of Pharaoh were in the prison, but the important thing is that they are put where Joseph is. Joseph occupies a good position, even here in the prison. Everywhere he went, his ability was certainly recognized. "A man's gift maketh room for him, and bringeth him before great men" (Prov. 18:16). Certainly this was true for Joseph. And God is moving in his life with a very definite purpose.

> And the captain of the guard charged Joseph with them,
> and he served them: and they continued a season in
> ward [Gen. 40:4].

Joseph got acquainted with them because he had charge of them. It was his business to take care of them while they were in prison.

> And they dreamed a dream both of them, each man his
> dream in one night, each man according to the interpre-
> tation of his dream, the butler and the baker of the king
> of Egypt, which were bound in the prison.
>
> And Joseph came in unto them in the morning, and
> looked upon them, and behold, they were sad [Gen.
> 40:5-6].

Joseph was an optimistic type of individual, always bright and sharp, and he finds these two fellows, who occupy positions with Pharaoh, sitting dolefully with very dark looks upon their faces.

> And he asked Pharaoh's officers that were with him in
> the ward of his lord's house, saying, Wherefore look ye
> so sadly today?
>
> And they said unto him, We have dreamed a dream, and
> there is no interpreter of it. And Joseph said unto them,
> Do not interpretations belong to God? tell me them, I
> pray you [Gen. 40:7-8].

Joseph gives God all the glory in this. Later on we will find another young Hebrew in a foreign court who will do the same thing—Daniel also gave God the glory. I wish Christians today would do this. Anything you or I do for the Lord should be done to the praise of God. Make sure that God gets the glory for it. I believe that one of the reasons many of us are not blessed as much as the Lord would like to bless us is because when we do receive something wonderful, we take it for granted and we do not give God the glory for it. We need to give

God the glory. Joseph should give God the glory, and he does! He says, "Do not interpretations belong to God?"

> **And the chief butler told his dream to Joseph, and said to him, In my dream, behold, a vine was before me;**
>
> **And in the vine were three branches: and it was as though it budded, and her blossoms shot forth; and the clusters thereof brought forth ripe grapes:**
>
> **And Pharaoh's cup was in my hand: and I took the grapes, and pressed them into Pharaoh's cup, and I gave the cup into Pharaoh's hand.**
>
> **And Joseph said unto him, This is the interpretation of it: The three branches are three days:**
>
> **Yet within three days shall Pharaoh lift up thine head, and restore thee unto thy place: and thou shalt deliver Pharaoh's cup into his hand, after the former manner when thou wast his butler [Gen. 40:9–13].**

It is interesting to see that God used dreams in the Old Testament. We don't find God moving that way in the New Testament, because then the canon of Scripture was complete. We don't need dreams today, but in that day, God did speak in dreams, and He used symbols that were meaningful to them. A butler would understand about serving wine—that was what he did for Pharaoh. Later on we will find King Nebuchadnezzar has a dream of an image. Now he was certainly acquainted with images and with idols—that would be something that he could understand very well.

Joseph was able to interpret the dream and promised the butler that he would be restored in three days.

> **But think on me when it shall be well with thee, and show kindness, I pray thee, unto me, and make mention of me unto Pharaoh, and bring me out of this house [Gen. 40:14].**

He says, "Now you will be out of here in three days, but I'll be here until I rot unless somebody moves in my behalf. I've interpreted your dream—please don't forget me!"

Now he gives him something of his background—

> **For indeed I was stolen away out of the land of the Hebrews: and here also have I done nothing that they should put me into the dungeon [Gen. 40:15].**

Although the record doesn't tell us, the butler probably promised that he would speak to Pharaoh in Joseph's behalf.

> **When the chief baker saw that the interpretation was good, he said unto Joseph, I also was in my dream, and, behold, I had three white baskets on my head:**
>
> **And in the uppermost basket there was of all manner of bakemeats for Pharaoh; and the birds did eat them out of the basket upon my head [Gen. 40:16–17].**

The dream of the baker is in a symbol meaningful to him. He can understand a basket filled with little cookies, sweetmeats.

> **And Joseph answered and said, This is the interpretation thereof: The three baskets are three days:**
>
> **Yet within three days shall Pharaoh lift up thy head from off thee, and shall hang thee on a tree; and the birds shall eat thy flesh from off thee [Gen. 40:18–19].**

Joseph's interprets his dream for him but warns that it is not going to be good for him. In three days he is to be taken out and hanged, and the birds will eat his flesh.

FULFILLMENT OF THE DREAMS

> **And it came to pass the third day, which was Pharaoh's birthday, that he made a feast unto all his servants: and**

he lifted up the head of the chief butler and of the chief baker among his servants.

And he restored the chief butler unto his butlership again; and he gave the cup into Pharaoh's hand:

But he hanged the chief baker: as Joseph had interpreted to them.

Yet did not the chief butler remember Joseph, but forgat him [Gen. 40:20–23].

Poor Joseph! This seems like a hopeless predicament now. Here he is, not only a slave, but one who has been falsely accused. Believe me, the prison bars are just as real as if he were guilty of some crime. The poor boy is here, and it is the purpose of Potiphar to forget him. That is his way of covering up the scandal that was in his own home. Joseph has to pay for Potiphar's cover-up. Joseph's one glimmer of light had been that the butler would remember him to Pharaoh. This seemed to be such a marvelous way of getting the ear of Pharaoh. But the butler is so elated with going back to his job and being in favor with Pharaoh again that he forgets all about poor Joseph. God wants to leave him there for a purpose. Suppose the butler had said to Pharaoh, "There is a prisoner down there who is innocent. He should not be there—he has been falsely accused. And he interpreted my dream for me. I sure would appreciate it, Pharaoh, if you would let him out." Suppose Pharaoh had let him out, don't you see what would have happened? He would have been at home in the land of Canaan at the time that Pharaoh needed him to interpret his dream. God wants to keep him nearby, and prison is a convenient place to keep him—there will be no difficulty in Pharaoh's finding him when he needs him.

In spite of the discouragement, Joseph believed that God was moving in his life, and there were fruits of faith which were apparent. He was faithful in every relationship of his life. He was faithful to Potiphar. In prison he was faithful to the keeper of the prison. He was faithful to God, always giving Him the glory. We will see later on that he will be faithful to Pharaoh, and he will be faithful to his own brothers. You see, Joseph's faith made him faithful. My friend, I believe that if you are truly a believer, you will be faithful.

We are living in a day when one of the tragic things happening is that there are so few Christians one can depend upon. I have a friend who is the head of a large Christian organization. We had a chance to sit together alone in a foreign city, just he and I. He was telling me some of the problems he had. He is in a tremendous organization, and yet he was telling me how few men he could really trust in his organization. Remember, this is a *Christian* organization. We see so few men in true faithfulness to their positions. We thank God for those who are. I have always thanked the Lord that He has put around me, everywhere I have ever been, a few faithful ones. I tell you, they are dear ones who are a great encouragement.

Joseph was that kind of a man. His faith made him faithful. It also gave him his optimistic outlook on life, even under all his trials and temptations. And it was faith that gave him his sympathetic and kindly attitude toward everyone. Notice how kind he was to the butler and the baker. And later on we will see his kindness to his brothers. Another thing that his faith did for him was to make him a very humble man. He gave God the glory for all his achievements. What a wonderful person he was! And what was responsible? Well, he *believed* God. He believed God as his father Abraham had believed Him, and this was the fruit that faith produced in his life.

Here is Joseph—forgotten in the prison. But Someone has not forgotten him; God has not forgotten him, and He is at work in his life.

Friend, this has a message for you and me. I don't know what your circumstances are right now, but I do know, judging from the letters that I get, that many folk are in a hard place. One man wrote to me, "I am between a rock and a hard place. Things look very dark." You don't see the way out, and you wonder if God cares. That is the reason God has given this story of Joseph. He wants you to know that He cares and that He is moving in your life. If you are His child, He is permitting things to happen to you for your own good. His chastisements are always for our good. Friend, we can't miss! How wonderful our God is!

CHAPTER 41

THEME: The dreams of Pharaoh; Joseph is made overseer of Egypt; Joseph's two sons—Manasseh and
Ephraim

What a difference this chapter is from the previous one where we
left Joseph down in jail, forgotten, forlorn, and forsaken. Yet all
of this was happening to him for God's purpose in his life. If we could
recognize God's hand in our lives today, it would give us a different
outlook on life! In the chapter before us we will see that Joseph is
released from prison when he interprets the dreams of Pharaoh. He is
made overseer over the entire land of Egypt, and he marries Asenath,
the daughter of the Priest of On, who bears him Manasseh and
Ephraim.

This is a story of rags to riches. I know of no fictitious story more
thrilling than this episode in the life of Joseph. In this chapter we can
certainly see the hand of God in his life. And Joseph was conscious of
God's care even during the days of adversity. This developed in him
many virtues which are the fruit of the Spirit. One of them was patience. The truth expressed in Romans 5:3 that tribulation (or trouble)
worketh patience is definitely illustrated in the life of Joseph.

We find here that this boy is brought into the presence of Pharaoh,
the gentile king, just as later on Daniel will be brought in before Nebuchadnezzar. Both of them are to interpret dreams.

Then we will consider the famine at the end of the chapter. What
purpose of God is to be accomplished by this? God will use it to get
the family of Jacob out of Canaan, away from the sins of the Canaanites
and to bring them to Egypt to settle in the secluded spot of Goshen.
That is one of His objectives. God had, I am sure, many other reasons,
but this one is obvious.

As we go along, I hope you are still taking note of the ways in
which Joseph is like the Lord Jesus Christ. We will make more of these
comparisons later on. It is something important for us to be noting.

THE DREAMS OF PHARAOH

Remember that in the previous chapter Pharaoh's butler and baker were put in the same prison where Joseph was incarcerated. Joseph interpreted their dreams correctly—the baker was hanged, and the butler was restored to his position. Joseph had begged the butler to remember his plight and speak of it to Pharaoh, but he had not done so. Now God gives Pharaoh a dream—

> **And it came to pass at the end of two full years, that Pharaoh dreamed: and, behold, he stood by the river [Gen. 41:1].**

Notice that it has been two full years since the close of the previous chapter. Joseph has spent two more years in jail, waiting for something to happen.

Here is Pharaoh's dream—

> **And, behold, there came up out of the river seven well favoured kine and fatfleshed; and they fed in a meadow.**
>
> **And, behold, seven other kine came up after them out of the river, ill favoured and leanfleshed; and stood by the other kine upon the brink of the river [Gen. 41:2-3].**

"Kine" are cows. We are talking about cattle here. He saw seven cows that were well-fed, fine-looking, fat cattle. Then he saw seven really skinny cows.

> **And the ill favoured and leanfleshed kine did eat up the seven well favoured and fat kine. Pharaoh awoke [Gen. 41:4].**

Pharaoh woke up and wondered what the dream meant. He didn't have the interpretation, but there was nobody to help him that day.

And he slept and dreamed the second time: and, behold, seven ears of corn came up upon one stalk, rank
and good.

And, behold, seven thin ears and blasted with the east
wind sprung up after them.

And the seven thin ears devoured the seven rank and
full ears. And Pharaoh awoke, and, behold, it was a
dream.

And it came to pass in the morning that his spirit was
troubled; and he sent and called for all the magicians of
Egypt, and all the wise men thereof: and Pharaoh told
them his dream; but there was none that could interpret
them unto Pharaoh [Gen. 41:5-8].

While all of these magicians and wise men were called in and Pharaoh was telling them his dream, the chief butler was there listening.
After all, his position was to stand before Pharaoh and get him anything that he wanted. When none of the wise men could give Pharaoh
an interpretation, the butler spoke up—

Then spake the chief butler unto Pharaoh, saying, I do
remember my faults this day [Gen. 41:9].

I would call it a little more than a "fault!" It was a sin, in my opinion.
But, you see, all of this was in the providence of God. We would call
them the fortuitous concurrence of circumstances. The difficult experiences of Joseph could not be understood at the time, but God was
letting them happen for a purpose. Now the chief butler says, "Oh, I
just remembered that I promised a young fellow down there in prison
that I would speak to you about him. And, by the way, Pharaoh, he can
interpret dreams." Now he tells Pharaoh his own experience—

Pharaoh was wroth with his servants, and put me in
ward in the captain of the guard's house, both me and
the chief baker:

> And we dreamed a dream in one night, I and he; we
> dreamed each man according to the interpretation of his
> dream.
>
> And there was with us a young man, an Hebrew, servant
> to the captain of the guard; and we told him, and he
> interpreted to us our dreams; to each man according to
> his dream he did interpret.
>
> And it came to pass, as he interpreted to us, so it was;
> me he restored unto mine office, and him he hanged
> [Gen. 41:10–13].

Pharaoh said, "Well, we've tried everybody else around here, and since that young man interpreted your dream and that of the baker, let's have him come because I have the feeling that my dreams are very significant."

> Then Pharaoh sent and called Joseph, and they brought
> him hastily out of the dungeon: and he shaved himself,
> and changed his raiment, and came in unto Pharaoh
> [Gen. 41:14].

Note that Joseph shaved himself. You must remember that the Hebrews were not shaving in that day. But have you noticed that the statues and paintings of the Egyptians show a cleanshaven people? Many of the rulers sported a little goatee to add dignity to their position—if they couldn't grow their own, they wore a false one—but generally the Egyptians were without hair on their faces.

There is a tremendous message in this. This man is lifted up out of the prison now. He shaves, and changes his prison garb for proper court clothing. This is a new life that is before him. It is like a resurrection; he is raised up. Now he goes to the Gentiles. What a tremendous picture of Christ this gives to us here.

> And Pharaoh said unto Joseph, I have dreamed a
> dream, and there is none that can interpret it: and I have

> heard say of thee, that thou canst understand a dream to interpret it [Gen. 41:15].

Notice how Joseph gives God the glory—

> And Joseph answered Pharaoh, saying, It is not in me: God shall give Pharaoh an answer of peace [Gen. 41:16].

From Joseph's viewpoint, God must receive the glory. Again let me say that the child of God should be very careful that God gets the glory for all of His accomplishments. If what we do is a blessing, it is because God is doing it through us. Joseph is aware of this, and he says, "It is not in me—I can't interpret it—but God shall give Pharaoh an answer of peace."

Pharaoh repeats the dreams to Joseph. Actually, it is one dream of two parts, and it is treated as a single dream.

> And Joseph said unto Pharaoh, The dream of Pharaoh is one: God hath shewed Pharaoh what he is about to do [Gen. 41:25].

Joseph says that the dream is one—both speak of the same thing. And the fact that it was repeated, given to Pharaoh twice, adds to its importance. The reason for the dream is that God is letting Pharaoh know what He is about to do. Here is the interpretation—

> The seven good kine are seven years; and the seven good ears are seven years: the dream is one.

> And the seven thin and ill favoured kine that came up after them are seven years; and the seven empty ears blasted with the east wind shall be seven years of famine.

> This is the thing which I have spoken unto Pharaoh: What God is about to do he sheweth unto Pharaoh.

> Behold, there come seven years of great plenty through-
> out all the land of Egypt:
>
> And there shall arise after them seven years of famine;
> and all the plenty shall be forgotten in the land of Egypt;
> and the famine shall consume the land;
>
> And the plenty shall not be known in the land by reason
> of that famine following; for it shall be very grievous
> [Gen. 41:26–31].

This, you see, is a prediction. There are to be seven years of plenty and
then seven years of famine.

> And for that the dream was doubled unto Pharaoh
> twice; it is because the thing is established by God, and
> God will shortly bring it to pass [Gen. 41:32].

The famine had been determined by God, and He wants Pharaoh to
know about it. Now here is the advice of Joseph to Pharaoh—

> Now therefore let Pharaoh look out a man discreet and
> wise, and set him over the land of Egypt.
>
> Let Pharaoh do this, and let him appoint officers over
> the land, and take up the fifth part of the land of Egypt
> in the seven plenteous years.
>
> And let them gather all the food of those good years that
> come, and lay up corn under the hand of Pharaoh, and
> let them keep food in the cities.
>
> And that food shall be for store to the land against the
> seven years of famine, which shall be in the land of
> Egypt; that the land perish not through the famine.
>
> And the thing was good in the eyes of Pharaoh, and in
> the eyes of all his servants [Gen. 41:33–37].

Joseph advises Pharaoh to collect all the surplus during the seven years of plenty and keep it in store for the lean years.

JOSEPH IS MADE OVERSEER OF EGYPT

And Pharaoh said unto his servants, Can we find such a one as this is, a man in whom the spirit of God is?

And Pharaoh said unto Joseph, Forasmuch as God hath shewed thee all this, there is none so discreet and wise as thou art:

Thou shalt be over my house, and according unto thy words shall all my people be ruled: only in the throne will I be greater than thou.

And Pharaoh said unto Joseph, See, I have set thee over all the land of Egypt [Gen. 41:38–41].

Notice the significance of this. At the beginning this boy had been in the back of the prison, forgotten, forsaken, and forlorn. Now he is brought out at the right psychological moment because nobody else can interpret the dream of Pharaoh. Not only does he interpret it, but in his enthusiasm and because he is a man of ability, he suggests what Pharaoh should do. God is leading him in all of this, of course.

There is to be a worldwide famine, a famine so severe that even Egypt will be affected. Because Egypt is an irrigated land, it is not dependent upon rainfall. The Upper Nile, the Blue Nile, comes down from Central Africa and furnishes the water upon which Egypt depends. Egypt gets about an inch of rainfall in a good year; so it is famine all the time as far as rainfall is concerned. But the Nile overflows the land every year, bringing not only water, but sediment which fertilizes the soil. However, God has warned that there will be seven years of famine which will affect Egypt, also.

As Pharaoh listens to Joseph, what he says makes sense. It is too bad that in my own nation there have not been men in our government who have had some sense of the future. Our foreign policy since the years before World War II, even from the days of Hitler's rise to power, has been more or less a first-aid program, something rushed in as an emergency measure. Someone once asked Gladstone what is the measure of a great statesman. He said it is the man who knows the direction God is going for the next fifty years. Well, here in Genesis, Pharaoh is told what is going to happen for the next fourteen years. Our nation could use a man like this, also.

Now, who could take over better than Joseph? Pharaoh recognized that he was a man of ability. Now don't you see how God had been training him in the home of Potiphar? We may wonder why in the world God ever let him go into that home in the first place. Now we realize that he had received quite a bit of training in the home of Potiphar where he had charge of everything the man owned. Now he is going to have charge of everything in the land of Egypt This is a tremendous transition in his life. He went all the way from the back of the jail to the throne next to that of Pharaoh.

> **And Pharaoh took off his ring from his hand, and put it upon Joseph's hand, and arrayed him in vestures of fine linen, and put a gold chain about his neck [Gen. 41:42].**

By the way, that ring had a signet on it. When that was put down in wax, it was just the same as Pharaoh's signature. Pharaoh is making Joseph his agent. He has the right to use the king's signature.

> **And he made him to ride in the second chariot which he had; and they cried before him, Bow the knee: and he made him ruler over all the land of Egypt.**

> **And Pharaoh said unto Joseph, I am Pharaoh, and without thee shall no man lift up his hand or foot in all the land of Egypt.**

> **And Pharaoh called Joseph's name Zaphnath-paaneah; and he gave him to wife Asenath the daughter of Potipherah priest of On. And Joseph went out over all the land of Egypt [Gen. 41:43–45].**

I like the name Joe better than I like *Zaphnath-paaneah*, but that was the name that Pharaoh gave to him. It is a Coptic name, and it means "the revealer of secret things."

And Joseph was thirty years old when he stood before Pharaoh king of Egypt. And Joseph went out from the presence of Pharaoh, and went throughout all the land of Egypt [Gen. 41:46].

We are told Joseph's age here, and we see that he has been in the land of Egypt for thirteen years. We know that two of those years were spent in prison after the episode with the butler and the baker. He probably had been in the prison a year or so before that. So he may have been in the house of Potiphar close to ten years. This gives us some idea of how his life was divided into time periods while he was in the land of Egypt.

After these thirteen years in Egypt, Joseph finds himself in a position which would correspond, I believe, to prime minister. He was second only to Pharaoh in the land of Egypt. Have you ever wondered why Pharaoh was so willing to accept him? Primarily, of course, the answer is that God was with him. All the way along we have been seeing that. The hand of God, by His providence, was leading this man. Joseph says himself that the brothers meant it for evil but that God meant it for good. It is wonderful to know that.

There may be another very practical reason for Pharaoh's accepting Joseph so readily. Many scholars hold that the Pharaoh at this particular time in history was one of the Hyksos kings. The Hyksos were not native Egyptians but were Bedouins from the Arabian Desert. They were a nomadic group, and for a period they came in and took over the throne of Egypt. If this is true (and I think it is), Pharaoh was actually closer in nationality to Joseph than to the Egyptians, and this gave him confidence in Joseph. Actually, these Hyksos kings found it a little difficult to find someone in Egypt who would be loyal and faithful to them. Faithfulness was certainly characteristic of Joseph. His confidence that God was moving in his life produced in him a faithfulness to whomever he was attached. He was faithful to his task because he knew that God was in it. A racial bond with Pharaoh may well be a reason that Joseph found such a ready reception with him at this time, and he certainly proved to be faithful to him, as we shall see.

By the way, the Hyksos kings were later expelled from Egypt, which I believe to be the reason that in Exodus 1:8 we read: "Now there arose up a new king over Egypt, which knew not Joseph." The Pharaoh of the oppression certainly had no fellow-feeling with the Hebrews!

Note that Pharaoh placed a chain about Joseph's neck, which gave him the same authority that Pharaoh had. Also, Pharaoh gave him for a bride the daughter of the priest of On. Her name, *Asenath*, means "dedicated to Neith (the Egyptian Minerva)." Evidently she came right out of heathenism.

This event in Joseph's life furnishes another parallel in the life of the Lord Jesus. Joseph had a gentile bride, and the Lord Jesus Christ is presently calling out of this world a gentile bride, which we call the church.

And in this same verse there is still another parallel; Joseph stood before Pharaoh when he was thirty years old, and the Lord Jesus began His ministry when He was thirty years of age. So at thirty, Joseph takes up his work in Egypt. During these seven years of plenty, he is gathering into storehouses the abundant produce of the land.

And in the seven plenteous years the earth brought forth by handfuls.

And he gathered up all the food of the seven years, which were in the land of Egypt, and laid up the food in the cities: the food of the field, which was round about every city, laid he up in the same [Gen. 41:47–48].

Notice that he "laid up the food in the cities." He was planning ahead for easy distribution. I remember that during the depression of the 1930s men stood in the lines of the soup kitchens of Chicago and New York, and the lines were blocks long. Although at that time there was an abundance of food, there was a problem of distribution. But Joseph is doing a very practical thing. He is laying up the food in the cities. He is gathering up the surplus, and he is putting it in the cities, ready for distribution.

> **And Joseph gathered corn as the sand of the sea, very much, until he left numbering; for it was without number [Gen. 41:49].**

Egypt was the breadbasket of the world. Under Joseph's management, I tell you, it seemed like two or three breadbaskets!

JOSEPH'S TWO SONS—MANASSEH AND EPHRAIM

Now we pause for a little family note—

> **And unto Joseph were born two sons before the years of famine came, which Asenath the daughter of Potipherah priest of On bare unto him.**
>
> **And Joseph called the name of the first born Manasseh: For God, said he, hath made me forget all my toil, and all my father's house.**
>
> **And the name of the second called he Ephraim: For God hath caused me to be fruitful in the land of my affliction [Gen. 41:50–52].**

These boys were born before the famine. He called his first son Manasseh. I'd say a good name for him would be "Amnesia" because it means that God had made Joseph "forget." He was so much involved that he forgot about his father's house. He'd been a homesick boy at first, but he's not anymore.

In the first part of this chapter we saw that Joseph, when he was released from prison, changed his clothes and shaved himself before appearing before Pharaoh. It may seem to you that shaving may not be very important, that only the Gillette Company would be interested in that fact. But to us it has a symbolic interest. The Hebrews wore beards, and when Joseph shaved himself and changed his clothing, it speaks to me of resurrection because he laid aside the old life and began the new life. From that point on, he dresses like an Egyptian; he talks like an Egyptian; he lives like an Egyptian. He says "God made me forget." So he names his son Manasseh—and you may call him Amnesia if you want to!

The next boy he names *Ephraim* because that means "fruitful." So you can call this next boy "Ambrosia" if you like. Someone may object that this is free translating. Maybe it is, but if you put those two boys' names into their English counterparts, that is exactly what they are. His boys were Amnesia and Ambrosia. Joseph gave them these names because God had made him forget his father's house and had made him fruitful in the land of Egypt.

And the seven years of plenteousness, that was in the land of Egypt, were ended [Gen. 41:53].

The seven years of bountiful crops are over now, and the famine will begin. At this time Joseph is thirty-seven years old. Keep that in mind for the next chapter.

And the seven years of dearth began to come, according as Joseph had said: and the dearth was in all lands; but in all the land of Egypt there was bread.

And when all the land of Egypt was famished, the people cried to Pharaoh for bread: and Pharaoh said unto all the Egyptians, Go unto Joseph; what he saith to you, do [Gen. 41:54–55].

May I call your attention to the fact that Joseph is the one who had the bread. There is another parallel here. Jesus Christ said, "I am the Bread of life."

And the famine was over all the face of the earth: and Joseph opened all the storehouses, and sold unto the Egyptians; and the famine waxed sore in the land of Egypt.

And all countries came into Egypt to Joseph for to buy corn; because that the famine was so sore in all lands [Gen. 41:56–57].

Notice that the famine is worldwide.

CHAPTER 42

THEME: Jacob sends ten sons to Egypt; Simeon left as hostage; nine brothers return home

The dramatic incidents in the life of Joseph are beginning to unfold. The pattern of God in using Joseph to preserve the race during the famine and the removal of Jacob and his sons to Egypt begins to emerge in clear detail. When Joseph was back in that dungeon, he couldn't see all of this. But he believed God. He is a man, who, because of his faith, was always enthusiastic and optimistic. Frankly, I wish my faith would get down far enough into shoe leather so that regardless of what happened, and regardless of what the circumstances are, I could be optimistic. I tell you, it doesn't take much rain or many dark clouds to make me less optimistic than I should be. I'm sure that is true of many of us today.

Joseph is in a unique position. I think you could almost guess what is going to happen. The famine is over all the earth, and all the earth is coming to Egypt to get grain. Guess who's coming to dinner!

The famine forces Jacob to send his ten sons to Egypt to buy food. Why only ten? Why didn't he send Benjamin? It would have killed him to have lost Benjamin.

Joseph recognized his brothers, but they did not recognize Joseph. Why not? Well, there are several reasons. First of all, they thought he was dead; so they were not looking for him at all. They never expected to see him again, but he did expect to see them.

Then, we must remember that many years had gone by. He was seventeen when they sold him, and now he is thirty-seven years old, plus however many years the famine has been going on. Let's say it was one year; so they hadn't seen him in twenty-one years. He's almost forty and he is dressed like an Egyptian, speaks and acts like an Egyptian.

But we are getting ahead of our story—

JACOB SENDS TEN SONS TO EGYPT

Now when Jacob saw that there was corn in Egypt, Jacob said unto his sons, Why do ye look one upon another? [Gen. 42:1].

They were looking at each other in a doleful way, not knowing where to turn or what to do.

And he said, Behold, I have heard that there is corn in Egypt: get you down thither, and buy for us from thence; that we may live, and not die [Gen. 42:2].

This illustrates faith. A great many people say that faith is so mysterious to them and that they don't know *how* to believe. I talked to a man who did not want to believe, but his argument was, "Well, how can I believe?" Notice here how Jacob believed. He heard something: "I have *heard* that there is corn in Egypt." He believed it, believed that it would bring life to them. So he acted upon his belief: "Get you down thither, and buy for us from thence; that we may live, and not die." My friend, that is what saving faith is. Some folk ask, "How can I believe in Jesus?" Can you imagine Jacob standing there before his ten sons and saying, "I've heard that there is corn down in Egypt, but how am I going to believe it?" Well, the way to believe it is to act upon it. The Bible says, ". . . *Believe* on the Lord Jesus Christ, and thou shalt be saved . . ." (Acts 16:31). You hear something and you believe it. That is what old Jacob did. That is the way he got corn which brought life to his family. And the way you and I get eternal life is through faith in Christ.

And Joseph's ten brethren went down to buy corn in Egypt.

But Benjamin, Joseph's brother, Jacob sent not with his brethren; for he said, Lest peradventure mischief befall him [Gen. 42:3–4].

Suppose mischief befalls the other ten boys, then what? Well, for one thing they are older. But if you want to know the truth, it wouldn't hurt Jacob as much as to lose Benjamin. Benjamin and Joseph were Rachel's boys, and Rachel was the wife he had deeply loved. And now he sends out all ten and keeps only Benjamin with him.

And the sons of Israel came to buy corn among those that came: for the famine was in the land of Canaan [Gen. 42:5].

Now we come to this dramatic moment—

And Joseph was the governor over the land, and he it was that sold to all the people of the land: and Joseph's brethren came, and bowed down themselves before him with their faces to the earth [Gen. 42:6].

Joseph has been watching for them. He knew they would have to come. There had been delegations there from all over the inhabited earth of that day. The famine was worldwide. So he watches, and lo and behold, here come the ten men. They all bow down before him. They got right down on their faces before Joseph. You wonder how he felt. By the way, what do you think of? Here is the literal fulfillment of the dreams of Joseph. Do you remember how he had dreamed as a boy that all the sheaves bowed down to his sheaf? Here it is taking place— all his older brothers are down on their faces before him.

And Joseph saw his brethren, and he knew them, but made himself strange unto them, and spake roughly unto them; and he said unto them, Whence come ye? And they said, From the land of Canaan to buy food.

And Joseph knew his brethren, but they knew not him [Gen. 42:7–8].

Do you know why he treated them roughly? He is testing them. We will find that he is going to test them all the way through. He is going to ask them some penetrating questions.

> **And Joseph remembered the dreams which he dreamed of them, and said unto them, Ye are spies; to see the nakedness of the land ye are come.**
>
> **And they said unto him, Nay, my lord, but to buy food are thy servants come.**
>
> **We are all one man's sons; we are true men, thy servants are no spies [Gen. 42:9-11].**

Believe me, Joseph is pouring it on—

> **And he said unto them, Nay, but to see the nakedness of the land ye are come.**
>
> **And they said, Thy servants are twelve brethren, the sons of one man in the land of Canaan; and, behold, the youngest is this day with our father, and one is not [Gen. 42:12-13].**

He is trying to get as much information as he can about his family without letting them know who he is. He accuses them of being spies.

There are only ten men there before him. They confess that they are really twelve and that one is home with their father. The other "is not" is what they think. In other words, they consider Joseph dead, but there he is standing before them!

Now for the third time Joseph accuses them of being spies.

> **And Joseph said unto them, That is it that I spake unto you, saying, Ye are spies:**
>
> **Hereby ye shall be proved: By the life of Pharaoh ye shall not go forth hence, except your youngest brother come hither.**

Send one of you, and let him fetch your brother, and he shall be kept in prison, that your words may be proved, whether there be any truth in you: or else by the life of Pharaoh surely ye are spies [Gen. 42:14–16].

Joseph is attempting to make contact with his youngest brother. These men are really half-brothers of his, but Benjamin is his full-brother, and he wants to see him. This is the way he attempts to accomplish this.

And he put them all together into ward three days [Gen. 42:17].

He locked them up in the town bastille.

Things look bad for them now, and they wonder what is going to happen.

And Joseph said unto them the third day, This do, and live; for I fear God [Gen. 42:18].

If there was anything that should have given the brothers an inkling of an idea who Joseph was, this statement was it. He says, "I fear God." Apparently in that day there were people other than just Jacob and his family who knew God. They knew that the way to God was by sacrifice. However, this sort of thing probably would not have excited the interest of these brethren. Maybe it even made them a little suspicious of this man. At least he gave a testimony for God. I want you to note that Joseph never misses an opportunity to give a testimony for God. Certainly he is giving one here. He always gives God the glory as the One who is directing his life. At least the statement that he fears God should have encouraged the brothers to believe that they would be treated justly at his hand.

If ye be true men, let one of your brethren be bound in the house of your prison: go ye, carry corn for the famine of your houses:

> But bring your youngest brother unto me; so shall your
> words be verified, and ye shall not die. And they did so
> [Gen. 42:19–20].

These brothers are men, some of them being over fifty years old, and
now they find themselves in a real predicament. They are being dealt
with by one who fears God, but they are afraid because they don't
know what he is going to do. Joseph makes the pretext of testing them
to see whether they are true men, but what he really wants is for his
younger brother to come the next time.

> And they said one to another, We are verily guilty con-
> cerning our brother, in that we saw the anguish of his
> soul, when he besought us, and we would not hear;
> therefore is this distress come upon us [Gen. 42:21].

What is taking place here is quite interesting. They are speaking in
Hebrew, and Joseph can understand them. Joseph had been speaking
to them through an interpreter. He didn't need to, but he did because
he is posing as an Egyptian. They are making a real confession of their
guilt.

> And Reuben answered them, saying, Spake I not unto
> you, saying, Do not sin against the child; and ye would
> not hear? therefore, behold, also his blood is required
> [Gen. 42:22].

They feel that what is happening to them is the vengeance of God
upon them for the way they treated Joseph.

SIMEON LEFT AS HOSTAGE

> And they knew not that Joseph understood them; for he
> spake unto them by an interpreter.

And he turned himself about from them, and wept; and returned to them again, and communed with them, and took from them Simeon, and bound him before their eyes [Gen. 42:23–24].

They say that this evil thing is coming upon them because of the evil they had done to Joseph. They are really repentant now. Joseph hears every bit of it, and he is moved toward them. He would love to walk up to them, throw his arms around each one of them, and call them "brother." But he dares not do it because he would never get Benjamin there.

He gives them a real test now. They must leave one of the brothers, and it is Simeon who is to stay. Joseph was so moved, so emotionally charged by all this that he had to weep. But he goes aside and washes his face; then comes in again as if nothing has happened.

I don't have any idea why they chose Simeon. I take it that while Joseph was gone out of the room, his brothers made the choice for Simeon to stay, and Joseph accepted that choice.

Then Joseph commanded to fill their sacks with corn, and to restore every man's money into his sack, and to give them provisions for the way: and thus did he unto them [Gen. 42:25].

He just couldn't take their money. So he not only gave them back their payment for the grain, but he gave them food for the trip home.

And they laded their asses with the corn, and departed thence.

And as one of them opened his sack to give his ass provender in the inn, he espied his money; for, behold, it was in his sack's mouth.

And he said unto his brethren, My money is restored; and, lo, it is even in my sack: and their heart failed

them, and they were afraid, saying one to another, What is this that God hath done unto us? [Gen. 42:26–28].

They feel that this is the judgment of God upon them. Ordinarily it would have been good news and a wonderful thing to have your money returned to you! Let me ask you this: Wouldn't you like to go down to your favorite supermarket to do your weekend grocery shopping, load up several of those great big carts and buy for your whole family; then wouldn't you like to open up your grocery sack at home and find that they had given you back all of the money you had paid for the groceries? Do you think that would be bad news to you? Especially, would it worry you if you learned that the grocer was giving this to you as a gift from him? Don't we all agree that under ordinary circumstances that would be good news? We would actually take it as an encouragement.

Well, it wasn't that for these men. They already feel that they are in hot water with this hard-boiled ruler down there in Egypt who has made it so difficult for them. This only adds to their concern.

We may wonder why they didn't go back to Egypt immediately. What would you have done under the circumstances? I think they feared they would really be in hot water had they gone back. Then this man would accuse them of stealing the money. They are not taking any chances. They are going on home, intending to bring the money back when they return.

NINE BROTHERS RETURN HOME

And they came unto Jacob their father unto the land of Canaan, and told him all that befell unto them; saying,

The man, who is the lord of the land, spake roughly to us, and took us for spies of the country.

And we said unto him, We are true men; we are no spies:

We be twelve brethren, sons of our father; one is not, and the youngest is this day with our father in the land of Canaan.

And the man, the lord of the country, said unto us, Hereby shall I know that ye are true men; leave one of your brethren here with me, and take food for the famine of your households, and be gone:

And bring your youngest brother unto me: then shall I know that ye are no spies, but that ye are true men: so will I deliver you your brother, and ye shall traffic in the land [Gen. 42:29–34].

Remember that they have left Simeon down there in Egypt.

And it came to pass as they emptied their sacks, that, behold, every man's bundle of money was in his sack: and when both they and their father saw the bundles of money, they were afraid [Gen. 42:35].

They thought it was a trick, of course.

And Jacob their father said unto them, Me have ye bereaved of my children: Joseph is not, and Simeon is not, and ye will take Benjamin away: all these things are against me [Gen. 42:36].

Poor old Jacob! He's not the cocky individual we once knew, nor is he quite the man of faith that we shall see a little later. But he is growing. He is not bragging now but is very pessimistic. He says, "All these things are against me." His son, Joseph, would not have said such a thing, but Jacob is saying it. Joseph would have said the same thing that Paul wrote so many years later: "And we know that all things work together for good to them that love God, to them who are the called according to his purpose" (Rom. 8:28). "Being confident of this very thing, that he which hath begun a good work in you will perform it unto the day of Jesus Christ" (Phil. 1:6).

And Reuben spake unto his father, saying, Slay my two sons, if I bring him not to thee: deliver him into my hand, and I will bring him to thee again.

And he said, My son shall not go down with you; for his brother is dead, and he is left alone: if mischief befall him by the way in which ye go, then shall ye bring down my gray hairs with sorrow to the grave [Gen. 42:37–38].

Jacob's life was wrapped up in the life of this boy Benjamin. You see, Joseph was his favorite because he was the firstborn of his lovely Rachel. Now Joseph is gone, which is a heartbreak to him. Now he faces the chance that he may lose this other son of Rachel, and he says that if this takes place he will die. Very candidly, he would have. His life was absolutely tied up in the life of Benjamin. He is the son of his right hand. He is the walking stick for Jacob. Jacob leans on him. That is what he has been doing these past years; so Jacob says that he will not let him go down to Egypt. In the meantime, poor Simeon is down there cooling his heels in jail!

CHAPTER 43

THEME: *Jacob sends his sons to Egypt; the brothers are entertained in Joseph's home*

Due to the seriousness of the famine, the sons of Jacob are forced to return with Benjamin to Egypt where they again have an audience with Joseph and present Benjamin. Joseph does not make himself known unto them at this time.

This is doubtless the most dramatic chapter in the Book of Genesis. I know of nothing that is quite as moving as the appearance of Benjamin before Joseph. The thing that brings them down to the land again is the seriousness of the famine. If the famine had lifted, I think Simeon would have spent the rest of his life in jail down in the land of Egypt, at least until Joseph released him.

JACOB SENDS HIS SONS TO EGYPT

And the famine was sore in the land.

And it came to pass, when they had eaten up the corn, which they had brought out of Egypt, their father said unto them, Go again, buy us a little food [Gen. 43:1–2].

Jacob realized they would starve to death if they didn't go down to Egypt again.

And Judah spake unto him saying, The man did solemnly protest unto us, saying, Ye shall not see my face, except your brother be with you.

If thou wilt send our brother with us, we will go down and buy thee food:

> But if thou wilt not send him, we will not go down: for
> the man said unto us, Ye shall not see my face, except
> your brother be with you [Gen. 43:3–5].

"The man" is their brother Joseph, but they do not know it. He had
presented to them a cut-and-dried proposition, and they knew he
meant it. Judah tells his father very definitely, "If we go down there,
we *must* have Benjamin with us. You wouldn't send him before, but
there is no use going if he is not with us this time because the man
won't see us."

> And Israel said, Wherefore dealt ye so ill with me, as to
> tell the man whether ye had yet a brother?
>
> And they said, The man asked us straitly of our state,
> and of our kindred, saying, Is your father yet alive? have
> ye another brother? and we told him according to the
> tenor of these words: could we certainly know that he
> would say, Bring your brother down? [Gen. 43:6–7].

Poor old Jacob is really frustrated. He says, "Why in the world did you
tell the man in the first place that you even had another brother?" He
doesn't realize that Joseph knew it anyway. But Jacob wishes his sons
had kept their mouths shut.

> And Judah said unto Israel his father, Send the lad with
> me, and we will arise and go; that we may live, and not
> die, both we, and thou, and also our little ones.
>
> I will be surety for him; of my hand shalt thou require
> him: if I bring him not unto thee, and set him before
> thee, then let me bear the blame for ever [Gen. 43:8–9].

The brothers were really quite reasonable in their answer to their
father. They told him that they hadn't intended to tell "the man"
everything but that he kept probing them. He was going to get his

information and wouldn't stop until he did—we know that. Then Judah comes forward as a surety for Benjamin.

Friend, you and I have a Surety today, and He came from the tribe of Judah. The Lord Jesus took my place and became my Shepherd, took my place and took my penalty. I was not able to meet His standard. I was not able to come up to His level. But the Lord Jesus stepped in and became my Surety and gave His life for me. What a picture of Christ we have here!

> **For except we had lingered, surely now we had returned this second time [Gen. 43:10].**

Judah says, "If you had let Benjamin go, we would have been there and back home by this time."

> **And their father Israel said unto them, If it must be so now, do this; take of the best fruits in the land in your vessels, and carry down the man a present, a little balm, and a little honey, spices, and myrrh, nuts, and almonds [Gen. 43:11].**

You will notice here that the thing they lacked was grain. They lacked bread, the staff of life. Apparently they had honey, nuts, and spices. So Jacob says they should send the man a gift. "Let's get on the sweet side of him" is actually what he is saying with the gift.

> **And take double money in your hand; and the money that was brought again in the mouth of your sacks, carry it again in your hand; peradventure it was an oversight:**
>
> **Take also your brother, and arise, go again unto the man:**
>
> **And God Almighty give you mercy before the man, that he may send away your other brother, and Benjamin. If I**

be bereaved of my children, I am bereaved [Gen. 43:12–
14].

So old Jacob relinquishes Benjamin and lets him go along with his
older brothers.

Now the dramatic moment comes when they stand again before
Joseph.

**And the men took that present, and they took double
money in their hand, and Benjamin; and rose up, and
went down to Egypt, and stood before Joseph [Gen.
43:15].**

You can well imagine Joseph's emotion as his eye singled out Benjamin!

JOSEPH ENTERTAINS HIS BROTHERS

**And when Joseph saw Benjamin with them, he said to
the ruler of his house, Bring these men home, and slay,
and make ready; for these men shall dine with me at
noon.**

**And the man did as Joseph bade; and the man brought
the men into Joseph's house [Gen. 43:16–17].**

The reason for Joseph's inviting them to his home is obvious. He
wants to talk with them in the privacy of his own home.

**And the men were afraid, because they were brought
into Joseph's house; and they said, Because of the money
that was returned in our sacks at the first time are we
brought in; that he may seek occasion against us, and
fall upon us, and take us for bondmen, and our asses
[Gen. 43:18].**

These men are really panicky now. They can't imagine him inviting them to his home for any *good* purpose. He had dealt with them so harshly before, and now he is inviting them to lunch!

Again, here is something that under ordinary circumstances would be something to brag about. Wouldn't you brag if the President of the United States had invited you to the Blue Room, or, better yet, the dining room for dinner? You would think it was a wonderful privilege. Yet, for these men, such a privilege brings no joy whatsoever. You see, they have a guilt complex. They feel guilty about everything that happens because they are the ones who sold their brother. Guilt changes joy into misery. In their fears, they wonder and begin to speculate. Could this man be plotting to take them as slaves because of the money in the sacks? Well, *they* had not hesitated to make a slave of Joseph when they sold him to the Ishmeelites for slavery in Egypt.

> **And they came near to the steward of Joseph's house, and they communed with him at the door of the house.**
>
> **And said, O sir, we came indeed down at the first time to buy food:**
>
> **And it came to pass, when we came to the inn, that we opened our sacks, and, behold, every man's money was in the mouth of his sack, our money in full weight: and we have brought it again in our hand.**
>
> **And other money have we brought down in our hands to buy food: we cannot tell who put our money in our sacks [Gen. 43:19–22].**

They are beginning to apologize, explain, and plead. They even appeal to this man who is conducting them to Joseph's home—who evidently was an official.

> **And he said, Peace be to you, fear not: your God, and the God of your father, hath given you treasure in your**

**sacks: I had your money. And he brought Simeon out
unto them [Gen. 43:23].**

Apparently, this man, through the testimony of Joseph, had come to a
knowledge of the living and true God. I think that Joseph had at least
partially let him in on what was taking place. When he said, "I had
your money," I imagine that frightened the brothers all the more.

**And the man brought the men into Joseph's house, and
gave them water, and they washed their feet; and he
gave their asses provender [Gen. 43:24].**

Here we see the custom of footwashing again. We saw it in the life of
Abraham and then again down in the city of Sodom. It was the custom
of that day.

**And they made ready the present against Joseph came at
noon: for they heard that they should eat bread there.**

**And when Joseph came home, they brought him the
present which was in their hand into the house, and
bowed themselves to him to the earth [Gen. 43:25–26].**

Remember that old Jacob had told his sons to take a present to "the
man." Notice that they "bowed themselves to him to the earth." Again
the boyhood dreams of Joseph are being fulfilled.

**And he asked them of their welfare, and said, Is your
father well, the old man of whom ye spake? Is he yet
alive? [Gen. 43:27].**

This is a dramatic moment! Joseph is probably seated, not necessarily
on a throne, but on an elevation of prominence, as his brothers bow
before him. When they stand to their feet, Joseph looks them right in
the eye, and they look at him. Joseph asks, "Is your father well, the old
man of whom ye spake? Is he still alive?" You see, Joseph is acutely
interested because he is *his* father, also.

> And they answered, Thy servant our father is in good
> health, he is yet alive. And they bowed down their
> heads, and made obeisance [Gen. 43:28].

Here they go down on their faces again. I would love to have a picture
of this, wouldn't you? Benjamin is with them, and he goes down on
his face, too.

> And he lifted up his eyes, and saw his brother, Ben-
> jamin, his mother's son, and said, Is this your younger
> brother, of whom ye spake unto me? And he said, God
> be gracious unto thee, my son [Gen. 43:29].

Joseph looks at his brother Benjamin, "his mother's son." The others
are his half-brothers, but this boy is his full-brother, his mother's son.
He asks, "Is this your younger brother, of whom ye spake unto me?" I
suppose the brothers nodded. Joseph said to Benjamin, "God be gracious unto thee, my son." What a dramatic moment! And Joseph can't
contain his emotion—

> And Joseph made haste; for his bowels did yearn upon
> his brother: and he sought where to weep; and he en-
> tered into his chamber, and wept there [Gen. 43:30].

"His bowels did yearn upon his brother"—that is, he was deeply
moved, and his heart went out to him. I suppose he said to his brothers, "Excuse me for a moment—someone wants me on the telephone,"
and he got out of the room as quickly as he could. He went into his
own private quarters and he wept. After all these years, he sees his
own brother Benjamin. It has been about twenty-two years. Joseph is
almost forty now, and Benjamin is a young man.

> And he washed his face, and went out, and refrained
> himself, and said, Set on bread [Gen. 43:31].

This is a marvelous, wonderful picture of something that is yet to be fulfilled. I hope that you will see this. The prophet Zechariah tells us that Jesus Christ is going to make Himself known unto His brethren someday. They are going to ask Him about the piercing of His side and the nail prints in His hands. He is going to say to them in that day, "These I received in the house of My friends." Then they will recognize Him, and they will weep. He is the One who has provided salvation for them. He is the One who gave His life for their redemption. This is going to take place when the Lord Jesus comes back to the earth. He will be revealed to His brethren, the nation Israel. There will be a remnant there who will know Him. Many of His brethren did not believe on Him when He came the first time, but at that time they are going to know Him.

Likewise, the brothers of Joseph are the ones who delivered him into slavery. They sold him, got rid of him. But now he is going to make himself known to his brethren. Someday our Lord Jesus Christ is going to do just that.

My Christian friend, beware of anti-Semitism. Regardless of how blind the nation of Israel is or what they engage in today, and regardless if they are not all lovely people, it is still true that they are the brethren of our Lord. There is coming the day when He is going to make Himself known to them. It is a family affair. We had better let His family alone. No real Christian can engage in antiSemitism.

After Joseph had gone to his private quarters to weep, he regained control of his emotions, washed his face, and returned to his brothers. He said, "Let's eat."

And they set on for him by himself, and for them by themselves, and for the Egyptians, which did eat with him, by themselves: because the Egyptians might not eat bread with the Hebrews: for that is an abomination unto the Egyptians [Gen. 43:32].

There are several things about this meal that the brothers would have noticed had they not been so frightened. The first thing is that Joseph did not eat with the Egyptians. The Egyptians ate alone. Joseph was separate from them. The brothers may have thought this was simply because he was the brass, the head man in this particular place.

Now here is something else—

And they sat before him, the firstborn according to his birthright, and the youngest according to his youth: and the men marvelled one at another [Gen. 43:33].

Joseph arranged the place cards, and he put Reuben in his proper place, he put Benjamin in his proper place, and all the brothers were in their right order, according to their ages. They looked at each other in amazement and wondered how he knew all that.

And he took and sent messes unto them from before him: but Benjamin's mess was five times so much as any of theirs. And they drank, and were merry with him [Gen. 43:34].

Also notice that he served their places. I wish our Authorized Version had used another word here instead of "messes" because that sounds messy, but of course it means portions. And again, he just could not refrain from showing his affection for his own brother Benjamin, so that he gave him five times as much. Now that young man had been through a famine, and this was his first real meal for a long time.

"And they drank, and were merry with him." It was a glorious affair. And what a wonderful day it will be when Joseph finally reveals himself to his brethren.

CHAPTER 44

THEME: Joseph sends his brothers home; Judah volunteers to take Benjamin's place

Again, we have a wonderful and dramatic chapter before us. Joseph has something else up his sleeve when he sends his brothers away with the grain. He tests his brothers relative to their relationship and their affection to Benjamin and their father. Remember, they had sold him into slavery. Have they changed? Will they be willing to let Benjamin go into slavery to save themselves? He needs to satisfy his mind in this regard before he makes himself known to them. The test he uses here would give him absolute proof that his brothers would not repeat the episode that he had experienced at their hands.

Judah acts as the spokesman for the group, and he is brought into a wonderful picture here. He is willing to take the place of Benjamin, and his eloquent defense of Benjamin is one of the most moving passages in the Bible.

JOSEPH SENDS BROTHERS HOME

And he commanded the steward of his house, saying, Fill the men's sacks with food, as much as they can carry, and put every man's money in his sack's mouth.

And put my cup, the silver cup, in the sack's mouth of the youngest, and his corn money. And he did according to the word that Joseph had spoken.

As soon as the morning was light, the men were sent away, they and their asses.

And when they were gone out of the city, and not yet far off, Joseph said unto his steward, Up, follow after the men; and when thou dost overtake them, say unto them, Wherefore have ye rewarded evil for good?

Is not this it in which my lord drinketh, and whereby indeed he divineth? ye have done evil in so doing [Gen. 44:1–5].

Joseph sends them away, and the brothers start out, thinking everything is all right. They have no idea of the cup in the sack of Benjamin. But the steward of Joseph's house comes after them with specific instructions. When the brothers get out a little way, they are overtaken. Here comes a whole troop after them, and they are accused of taking the cup belonging to Joseph.

And he overtook them, and he spake unto them these same words.

And they said unto him, Wherefore saith my lord these words? God forbid that thy servants should do according to this thing [Gen. 44:6–7].

Note that the steward says that Joseph uses this cup for "divining." Remember that Joseph was a prophet, and he was able to foretell the future. We know that is so because he interpreted the dreams of the baker, the butler, and of Pharaoh. He may have used this cup, or maybe that was part of the ruse that he used. We must understand that his gift of prophecy was a gift that God had given him, and this was before there was any written revelation. We are not to get a cup and look at tea leaves, nor are we to watch the horoscope—that is all absolute nonsense. It reveals the sad spiritual condition of people today when they turn to that sort of thing. Joseph had a gift. It was not in the cup. His gift was from God.

Behold, the money, which we found in our sacks' mouths, we brought again unto thee out of the land of Canaan: how then should we steal out of thy lord's house silver or gold?

With whomsoever of thy servants it be found, both let him die, and we also will be my lord's bondmen [Gen. 44:8–9].

They were so sure that none of them had the cup.

> **And he said, Now also let it be according unto your words: he with whom it is found shall be my servant; and ye shall be blameless.**
>
> **Then they speedily took down every man his sack to the ground, and opened every man his sack.**
>
> **And he searched, and began at the eldest, and left at the youngest: and the cup was found in Benjamin's sack [Gen. 44:10–12].**

Of course, Joseph had instructed his steward to put the cup in Benjamin's sack.

> **Then they rent their clothes, and laded every man his ass, and returned to the city [Gen. 44:13].**

They "rent" or tore their clothes as a gesture of extreme distress. They all turned around to go back. They are not going home without Benjamin, you may be sure of that. Here they fall on the ground before Joseph again. This time it is in dismay and in agony—

> **And Judah and his brethren came to Joseph's house; for he was yet there: and they fell before him on the ground.**
>
> **And Joseph said unto them, What deed is this that ye have done? wot ye not that such a man as I can certainly divine? [Gen. 44:14–15].**

JUDAH VOLUNTEERS TO TAKE BENJAMIN'S PLACE

Judah comes to the front, and the nobility of this man really stands out now. Remember it is from the tribe of Judah that the Saviour is to come. This man makes one of the finest speeches ever recorded. He

makes a full confession that it is because of their sin that this has come
upon them.

> And Judah said, What shall we say unto my lord? what
> shall we speak? or how shall we clear ourselves? God
> hath found out the iniquity of thy servants: behold, we
> are my lord's servants, both we, and he also with whom
> the cup is found.
>
> And he said, God forbid that I should do so: but the man
> in whose hand the cup is found, he shall be my servant;
> and as for you, get you up in peace unto your father
> [Gen. 44:16–17].

Joseph wants to test them now in regard to their love for their brother.
He says that Benjamin is the guilty one; so it is Benjamin who must
stay. They had sold *him* into slavery; now he says, "Just leave Benjamin here, and he can be my slave. He is the guilty one. The rest of
you can go home." Now listen to Judah—

> Then Judah came near unto him, and said, Oh my lord,
> let thy servant, I pray thee, speak a word in my lord's
> ears, and let not thine anger burn against thy servant:
> for thou art even as Pharaoh [Gen. 44:18].

You can see the position which Joseph occupies in Egypt.

> My lord asked his servants, saying, Have ye a father, or
> a brother?
>
> And we said unto my lord, We have a father, an old man,
> and a child of his old age, a little one; and his brother is
> dead, and he alone is left of his mother, and his father
> loveth him.
>
> And thou saidst unto thy servants, Bring him down unto
> me, that I may set mine eyes upon him.

And we said unto my lord, The lad cannot leave his father: for if he should leave his father, his father would die.

And thou saidst unto thy servant, Except your youngest brother come down with you, ye shall see my face no more.

And it came to pass when we came up unto thy servant my father, we told him the words of my lord.

And our father said, Go again, and buy us a little food.

And we said, We cannot go down: if our youngest brother be with us, then will we go down: for we may not see the man's face, except our youngest brother be with us.

And thy servant my father said unto us, Ye know that my wife bare me two sons:

And the one went out from me, and I said, Surely he is torn in pieces; and I saw him not since:

And if ye take this also from me, and mischief befall him, ye shall bring down my gray hairs with sorrow to the grave [Gen. 44:19–29].

Judah here in this statement is recounting what has happened and the feelings of their father. Actually, the father had been deceived, and Joseph can see that now. He now knows exactly what the brothers told their father had happened to him so long ago. I believe that this is the first time any one of them has said that much. They had said previously that he "was not," meaning that he was dead.

We can see something else. Jacob is growing in grace, but he hasn't arrived. Instead of trusting the Lord, he is leaning on this boy Benjamin. If anything had happened to Benjamin, it would have killed him—he would have gone down into his grave, sorrowing.

There are Christians today who reveal a very wonderful faith in

God at the time when death comes to a loved one. Others actually collapse when this happens. I don't care how much you love a member of your family, friend, if you both are children of God, you know you are going to see each other again someday. The one walking by faith is not going to collapse at a time like that. Therefore, we can recognize that Jacob has not yet arrived. Although he is growing in grace, he still does not have a complete trust in God.

> **Now therefore when I come to thy servant my father, and the lad be not with us; seeing that his life is bound up in the lad's life;**

> **It shall come to pass, when he seeth that the lad is not with us, that he will die; and thy servants shall bring down the gray hairs of thy servant our father with sorrow to the grave [Gen. 44:30–31].**

You notice the concern that Judah has here for old Jacob. Judah is the spokesman for the group. I think any one of the other brothers would have made this same statement.

> **For thy servant became surety for the lad unto my father, saying, If I bring him not unto thee, then I shall bear the blame to my father for ever.**

> **Now therefore, I pray thee, let thy servant abide instead of the lad a bondman to my lord; and let the lad go up with his brethren.**

> **For how shall I go up to my father, and the lad be not with me? lest peradventure I see the evil that shall come on my father [Gen. 44:32–34].**

Again, Judah is the spokesman for the group, and any one of them would have offered himself. Joseph tests his brothers, and they all pass the test. Rather than to see Benjamin go into slavery, they are willing to take his place.

My friend, later on in history there came One in the line of Judah, the Lion of the tribe of Judah, who bore the penalty for the guilty. "... God commendeth his love toward us, in that, while we were yet sinners, Christ died for us" (Rom. 5:8). Christ took the place of the guilty.

CHAPTER 45

THEME: *Joseph reveals his identity; Joseph invites his family to Egypt*

The story from the previous chapters continues right on in the chapter before us. Joseph reveals himself to his brethren and identifies himself with them.

JOSEPH REVEALS HIS IDENTITY

Then Joseph could not refrain himself before all them that stood by him; and he cried, Cause every man to go out from me. And there stood no man with him, while Joseph made himself known unto his brethren [Gen. 45:1].

Joseph clears the room.

And he wept aloud: and the Egyptians and the house of Pharaoh heard [Gen. 45:2].

This time Joseph could not get out of the room. He just breaks down and begins to weep. No one knows why except Joseph. His own brethren at this time do not know, and the servants who are there do not know. Now there is no further reason for Joseph to conceal his identity from them, as he has fully tested his brethren.

Let me repeat that the day is coming when the Lord Jesus Christ is going to make Himself known unto His brethren, the Jews. When He came the first time, "he came unto his own, and his own received him not" (John 1:11). In fact, they delivered Him up to be crucified. But when He comes the second time, He will make Himself known to His own people. "And one shall say unto him, What are these wounds in thine hands? Then he shall answer, Those with which I was wounded in the house of my friends" (Zech. 13:6). Christ will make Himself known to His brethren. And "in that day there shall be a fountain opened to the house of David and to the inhabitants of Jerusalem for sin and for uncleanness" (Zech. 13:1). It will be a family affair between the Lord Jesus and His brethren. The episode of Joseph revealing himself to his brothers gives us a little inkling of how wonderful that day of Christ's revelation will be.

Joseph is so charged with emotion that he can't contain himself. In the house of Pharaoh they can hear the weeping. They can't understand what is happening over at Joseph's house.

> **And Joseph said unto his brethren, I am Joseph: doth my father yet live? And his brethren could not answer him; for they were troubled at his presence [Gen. 45:3].**

"Troubled" in our translation is really not strong enough. The brothers were *terrified* at his presence. I tell you, if you think they were afraid before, they were really terrified now. It had been close to twenty-five years since they had seen him when they sold him to the Ishmaelites, and they are sure that now he will want to get his revenge. They are too shocked and frightened to speak.

> **And Joseph said unto his brethren, Come near to me, I pray you. And they came near. And he said, I am Joseph your brother, whom ye sold into Egypt [Gen. 45:4].**

"I'm your brother." Here is a dramatic moment! Can you imagine how they feel? Notice the reaction of Joseph here. He is not angry, and he does not seek revenge. That would be the normal, human reaction. Then why doesn't he seek revenge?

> **Now therefore be not grieved, nor angry with yourselves, that ye sold me hither: for God did send me before you to preserve life [Gen. 45:5].**

You see, the thing that Joseph could see in all of this was that God had permitted it for a purpose. God was moving in his life.

> For these two years hath the famine been in the land: and yet there are five years, in the which there shall neither be earing nor harvest.
>
> And God sent me before you to preserve you a posterity in the earth, and to save your lives by a great deliverance.
>
> So now it was not you that sent me hither, but God: and he hath made me a father to Pharaoh, and lord of all his house, and a ruler throughout all the land of Egypt [Gen. 45:6–8].

If you and I could see the hand of God in our lives, would we become angry and seek revenge? I don't think we would. Again this man gives the glory to God.

Joseph was seventeen when he was brought into Egypt. He was thirty when he stood before Pharaoh. There had been seven years of plenty and now there have passed two years of famine. So Joseph is thirty-nine years old and has been living in the land of Egypt for twenty-two years. He sees the hand of God in all of this.

JOSEPH INVITES HIS FAMILY TO EGYPT

> Haste ye, and go up to my father, and say unto him, Thus saith thy son Joseph, God hath made me lord of all Egypt: come down unto me, tarry not:
>
> And thou shalt dwell in the land of Goshen, and thou shalt be near unto me, thou, and thy children, and thy children's children, and thy flocks, and thy herds, and all that thou hast:

> And there will I nourish thee; for yet there are five years
> of famine; lest thou, and thy household, and all that
> thou hast, come to poverty [Gen. 45:9–11].

Jacob and his family could not have survived had they stayed in the
land of Palestine at this particular time. They would have perished.
Joseph wants to bring them down to the land of Goshen which is actually the best part of Egypt. It is in that land that God is going to make
them a nation, sheltered from the rest of the world. The lives of the
brothers revealed that they needed to get out of the land of Canaan.

> And, behold, your eyes see, and the eyes of my brother
> Benjamin, that it is my mouth that speaketh unto you
> [Gen. 45:12].

I think that they stood there absolutely spellbound and were down
on their faces and then up again and that they had absolutely nothing to say as they listened to Joseph speaking words that seemed
unbelievable—they would have been unbelievable but Joseph was
right there before them.

> And ye shall tell my father of all my glory in Egypt, and
> of all that ye have seen; and ye shall haste and bring
> down my father hither.
>
> And he fell upon his brother Benjamin's neck, and
> wept; and Benjamin wept upon his neck [Gen. 45:13–
> 14].

This is a tender scene between these two full-brothers. Joseph and
Benjamin are both marvelous men.

> Moreover he kissed all his brethren, and wept upon
> them: and after that his brethren talked with him [Gen.
> 45:15].

The other brothers were stunned, but now they begin to recover their senses, and they have quite a talk.

And then the news begins to be spread abroad.

And the fame thereof was heard in Pharaoh's house, saying, Joseph's brethren are come: and it pleased Pharaoh well, and his servants [Gen. 45:16].

There was all this noise in the house of Joseph, and the people could hear it. Pharaoh wanted to know what was going on, and I suppose he asked one of the servants from Joseph's house what it all meant. The servant probably said, "Well, you know those eleven men who came down from Canaan—they're Joseph's *brothers!*" It delighted Pharaoh. Why would it delight him? Remember that Pharaoh was probably a Hyksos king and of the same racial strain as Joseph and his family. He hadn't been able to trust the Egyptians too much and was pleased with Joseph's faithfulness; so he was delighted that there were going to be more like him.

And Pharaoh said unto Joseph, Say unto thy brethren, This do ye; lade your beasts, and go, get you unto the land of Canaan;

And take your father and your households, and come unto me: and I will give you the good of the land of Egypt, and ye shall eat the fat of the land.

Now thou art commanded, this do ye; take you wagons out of the land of Egypt for your little ones, and for your wives, and bring your father, and come [Gen. 45:17–19].

Notice that Pharaoh orders wagons to be sent. The wheel was quite an invention, and these men from Canaan were not using wagons yet, but the Egyptians were more advanced.

> Also regard not your stuff; for the good of all the land of
> Egypt is yours [Gen. 45:20].

"You won't need to bring anything extra; we'll furnish everything you
need."

> And the children of Israel did so: and Joseph gave them
> wagons, according to the commandment of Pharaoh,
> and gave them provision for the way.

> To all of them he gave each man changes of raiment; but
> to Benjamin he gave three hundred pieces of silver, and
> five changes of raiment.

> And to his father he sent after this manner; ten asses
> laden with the goods things of Egypt, and ten she asses
> laden with corn and bread and meat for his father by the
> way.

> So he sent his brethren away, and they departed: and he
> said unto them, See that ye fall not out by the way.

> And they went up out of Egypt, and came into the land
> of Canaan unto Jacob their father.

> And told him, saying, Joseph is yet alive, and he is gov-
> ernor over all the land of Egypt. And Jacob's heart
> fainted, for he believed them not [Gen. 45:21–26].

He just could not believe it was true.

> And they told him all the words of Joseph, which he had
> said unto them: and when he saw the wagons which Jo-
> seph had sent to carry him, the spirit of Jacob their
> father revived [Gen. 45:27].

Finally old Jacob was convinced, and he began to exhibit some enthusiasm.

**And Israel said, It is enough; Joseph my son is yet alive:
I will go and see him before I die [Gen. 45:28].**

What thrilling developments we are seeing here! The prospect of seeing Joseph certainly influenced Jacob to make the decision to go down to Egypt. Do you think that he intended to remain in Egypt? I don't think so. I think he intended to pay a brief visit to his son and then return back home as soon as the famine was over. But he never returned to Canaan except for a burial, his own. He died in the land of Egypt. Although his whole family lived there, he was buried in the land of Canaan.

CHAPTER 46

THEME: Jacob and family move to Egypt; Jacob and Joseph reunited

Jacob probably thought he was going to Egypt for only a few years, and even then it was with some reluctance and hesitation that he consented going there. God had instructed Abraham to stay out of Egypt, and Abraham had been in trouble down there. God had said the same thing to Isaac. So now the question is, should Jacob go down into the land of Egypt? He needs a little more encouragement than the invitation from his son Joseph or even from Pharaoh. He needs to have a green light from God.

JACOB AND FAMILY MOVE TO EGYPT

And Israel took his journey with all that he had, and came to Beer-sheba, and offered sacrifices unto the God of his father Isaac [Gen. 46:1].

Here is the amazing thing: he offered sacrifices to the God of his father Isaac. The first time he left that land going to the land of Haran, he had come to Bethel. Was he looking for God? No, he thought he had run away from Him. He wasn't seeking the mind of God at all, nor was he asking for His leading. What a contrast there is between young Jacob and the servant of Abraham. The servant of Abraham never took a step without looking to God, but Jacob didn't think that he needed God in his life at all. It took a long time for him to learn that was not the proper way to go through life.

How many Christians today go through the entire week and leave God pretty much out of their program. They make their own decisions and do what they want to do. Then they come to church on Sunday, are very religious and are willing to do God's will—they think God's will for them is merely to go to church and maybe teach a Sunday school class. Then they tell God good-bye on Sunday night. The rest of the week God is not in the picture for them.

This man Jacob, for most of his life, had not been looking to God, but now, as he comes to Beersheba, he offers sacrifices unto the God of his father Isaac.

Now God is going to be gracious and appear to him—

> **And God spake unto Israel in the visions of the night, and said, Jacob, Jacob. And he said, Here am I.**

> **And he said, I am God, the God of thy father: fear not to go down into Egypt; for I will there make of thee a great nation [Gen. 46:2-3].**

Now God is promising that He will make of Jacob a great nation down in the land of Egypt. You may be wondering if God did that. We find the answer in the next book of the Bible: "And the children of Israel were fruitful, and increased abundantly, and multiplied, and waxed exceeding mighty; and the land was filled with them" (Exod. 1:7). There was a real population explosion of Israelites in the land of Egypt. What is the explanation of that? God is making good His promise to Jacob. "I am God, the God of thy Father: fear not to go down into Egypt: for I will there make of thee a great nation." God made good that which He promised to him.

> **I will go down with thee into Egypt; and I will also surely bring thee up again: and Joseph shall put his hand upon thine eyes.**

> **And Jacob rose up from Beer-sheba: and the sons of Israel carried Jacob their father, and their little ones, and their wives, in the wagons which Pharaoh had sent to carry him [Gen. 46:4-5].**

Pharaoh, you recall, had sent these wagons from Egypt. They put Jacob in one of the wagons, and off they go.

The life of Jacob can be divided into three geographical locations:

the land of Haran, the land of Canaan, and the land of Egypt. These are not only geographical areas, but they denote three spiritual levels. Jacob left the land with just a staff. When he came into Haran, he was God's man living in the flesh. He came out of Haran, running. He was running away from his father-in-law and was afraid to meet his own brother Esau. Then in the land of Canaan Jacob had his wrestling match, but he is God's man who is fighting in his own strength. Now he is going to Egypt. He is not walking in his own strength, and he is not running away anymore. He is now walking by faith.

Although Joseph is prominent in this section of Genesis, be sure to mark the evidences of the spiritual man of faith in the life of Jacob. Jacob has become the man that God wanted him to be, and only God can make this kind of man.

Let me state this again. Jacob's life in Haran typifies the man of God who is living in the flesh. Jacob's life in the land of Canaan typifies the man of God who is fighting in his own strength. Jacob's life in Egypt typifies the man of God who is walking by faith.

This, I believe, is true also for a great many of us today. There was that time in our lives when we came in contact with the gospel, the Word of God, and we turned to Him. Then there was that period of struggle when we thought we could live our lives in our own strength. Perhaps that lasted for years. Then there came the time when we did grow in grace and in the knowledge of our Lord Jesus Christ and began to walk by faith.

> **And they took their cattle, and their goods, which they had gotten in the land of Canaan, and came into Egypt, Jacob, and all his seed with him:**
>
> **His sons, and his sons' sons with him, his daughters, and his sons' daughters, and all his seed brought he with him into Egypt [Gen. 46:6–7].**

Because of the famine, Jacob had to take everyone—children and grandchildren. And all of their livestock had to go with them since none could have survived the famine.

The following verses give the geneaology of Jacob. It is very important because it is the genealogy which will lead to Jesus Christ and
will be followed through the rest of the Bible. After a list of all of
Jacob's descendants, we read this:

> **All the souls that came with Jacob into Egypt, which
> came out of his loins, besides Jacob's sons' wives, all the
> souls were threescore and six [Gen. 46:26].**

From Jacob there were sixty-six people who came with him from Canaan into Egypt. Of course, Joseph and his family were already in
Egypt—

> **And the sons of Joseph, which were born him in Egypt,
> were two souls: all the souls of the house of Jacob, which
> came into Egypt, were threescore and ten [Gen. 46:27].**

This brought the total household of Jacob to seventy souls.

Notice that each son of Jacob and his offspring are listed by name.
Why are these lists of names given to us in the Scriptures? Doesn't
God have more important information to give to us? My friend, there
is nothing more important than our Lord Jesus Christ, and this is the
genealogy that leads to Him. We will find some of these names in the
genealogy in the first chapter of Matthew, at the beginning of the New
Testament. Again, we will find some of these names in the genealogy
given to us in Luke, chapter 3. These lists of names are important for
that reason.

There is another reason, and it is very personal. Have you heard of
the Lamb's Book of Life? The question is: Is your name written there?
Just as you got into the line of Adam (and we all are in that line), you
get into the line of Christ—that is, by birth. But in the case of the
Lamb's Book of Life, you get there by the *new* birth which comes about
by receiving Christ as your personal Savior. When you do that, you
become a child of God.

How important are you? Well, I don't know you—probably have
never heard of you—but God knows you. In fact, He has numbered the

very hairs of your head! He knows you better than anyone else knows you. He knows you and loves you more than your mother ever did—I don't imagine that she ever counted the hairs of your head! God did. God knows you *personally*.

In Jacob's genealogy there are names that mean nothing to me. In watching the news on television, I saw the crowd of young folk at a rock festival, a mob of about two hundred thousand dirty, filthy folk. They may have needed a bath to begin with, but it had just rained, and they were covered with mud. As I looked at them, I thought, *God knows each one of them, and God loves each one. They are not thinking of Him, but each one is precious in God's sight, and Christ died for each one.* My friend, here you are in the midst of a great population explosion with literally millions of people around you, yet you are an individual to God. And the names listed in Jacob's genealogy are people whom I don't know. Candidly, I'm not interested in them. But God is. He delighted in putting their names down because they were His. This again causes me to ask you the question: Is your name written in the Lamb's Book of Life?

Now here comes Jacob with all of his family to the land of Egypt.

And he sent Judah before him unto Joseph, to direct his face unto Goshen; and they came into the land of Goshen [Gen. 46:28].

JACOB AND JOSEPH REUNITED

What a picture we have here—

And Joseph made ready his chariot, and went up to meet Israel his father, to Goshen, and presented himself unto him; and he fell on his neck, and wept on his neck a good while [Gen. 46:29].

Joseph fell on the neck of his father and embraced him, and he wept there. The Word of God says it was a good while. I don't know how long a "good while" is, but it does mean that it wasn't just a brisk handshake that had no meaning. The emotion was quite real. Oh, what a marvelous meeting this was!

> And Israel said unto Joseph, Now let me die, since I have seen thy face, because thou art yet alive [Gen. 46:30].

What a joy this was to old Jacob! Frankly, friend, I think that Jacob was an old man about ready to die. I believe he barely made this trip, but God sustained him. We will find that he is permitted to live for a few years in the land of Egypt. Israel and Joseph have these last years together. Notice that Jacob is now "the child of God who lives by faith." Therefore, he is called by his name *Israel*.

> And Joseph said unto his brethren, and unto his father's house, I will go up, and shew Pharaoh, and say unto him, My brethren, and my father's house, which were in the land of Canaan, are come unto me;
>
> And the men are shepherds, for their trade hath been to feed cattle; and they have brought their flocks, and their herds, and all that they have.
>
> And it shall come to pass, when Pharaoh shall call you, and shall say, What is your occupation?
>
> That ye shall say, Thy servants' trade hath been about cattle from our youth even until now, both we, and also our fathers; that ye may dwell in the land of Goshen; for every shepherd is an abomination unto the Egyptians [Gen. 46:31–34].

They had the same problem in Egypt in that day as we had in the western part of the United States. I remember when I was a boy in West Texas that, if a man tried to raise sheep in that area, he was in trouble. He found he didn't have any friends at all, and I mean he was in *real* trouble. Just so, the Egyptians didn't care for shepherds.

It is interesting that the Word of God has had so much to say about shepherds. These people were shepherds who raised their own sheep, and they still do in the land of Israel. "Shepherd" is the figure of speech which is used to describe our Lord. He is the Good Shepherd who gives His life for the sheep. He is the Great Shepherd of His sheep who watches over them today. He is the Chief Shepherd who is yet to appear. He calls Himself the Shepherd.

And, my friend, He is an abomination to the world. He is not received today. I am speaking of the real Jesus Christ. Liberalism has concocted a Jesus whom the world will accept. They have made an idol that doesn't even look like the Lord Jesus of the Bible. The one they talk about is not virgin-born; he never performed miracles; he did not die for the sins of the world; and he was not raised bodily from the dead. The Jesus of the liberal never lived. There is no record of a Jesus like that. The only One we have records of was virgin-born, performed miracles, died for the sins of the world, and arose bodily from the grave. That is the Shepherd whom the world doesn't like. He is still an abomination to the world.

Shepherds were an abomination to the Egyptians. Joseph tells his brothers to tell Pharaoh that they are shepherds and that they raise cattle. Actually, they had both cattle and sheep. We will find later that Pharaoh will give them the land of Goshen and will ask them to take care of his sheep so that the children of Israel became the shepherds in the land of Egypt.

It is really quite wonderful to see that now the family of Jacob is living in the land of Goshen. This is to be their home for a long time. After the death of Joseph, they will become slaves in the land of Egypt, but God will be with them through all that time. They will become a great nation down there, and then God will lead them out under Moses.

There is no record that God ever appeared to Joseph, yet we certainly see the providence of God in the life of Joseph. It is obvious to us now that he had to come ahead to prepare the way so that the entire family of Jacob could survive in the land of Egypt.

CHAPTER 47

THEME: Joseph presents father and brothers to Pharaoh; Joseph promises Jacob burial in Canaan

We have seen how Jacob and all his family have arrived in the land of Egypt. Joseph, as a move of strategy, brought them into the land of Goshen. This actually was the richest land in that day, but right now they are in the midst of a famine and no land is very valuable to the owner at this particular time.

We are going to find that this is the best chapter in the life of Jacob so far. Jacob doesn't appear in a good light when we first meet him in Scripture. In fact, not until he makes his trip to Egypt do we begin to see that he has become a man of faith. This chapter, more than any other, reveals that.

The famine becomes more intense as it draws to an end. Although all the people of the world are involved in this, Canaan and Egypt are the lands which are mentioned because they are the particular areas in the development of the story which is told to us here.

JOSEPH PRESENTS FATHER AND BROTHERS TO PHARAOH

Then Joseph came and told Pharaoh, and said, My father and my brethren, and their flocks, and their herds, and all that they have, are come out of the land of Canaan; and, behold, they are in the land of Goshen [Gen. 47:1].

Joseph is going to present his father and his brothers to the Pharaoh of Egypt. He put them in the land of Goshen before he asked for a place for them. You can see the strategy in that. If they were already there, Pharaoh would be more apt to give them that land. After all, they would already be moved in and have unpacked their goods.

> And he took some of his brethren, even five men, and
> presented them unto Pharaoh.
>
> And Pharaoh said unto his brethren, What is your oc-
> cupation? And they said unto Pharaoh, Thy servants
> are shepherds, both we, and also our fathers [Gen.
> 47:2–3].

We saw that shepherds and cattlemen didn't get along in those days.
Egyptians just didn't care for shepherds, neither did they care for
shepherding. So that opened up an opportunity for the children of
Israel to do something that the Egyptians would not want to do.

> They said moreover unto Pharaoh, For to sojourn in the
> land are we come; for thy servants have no pasture for
> their flocks; for the famine is sore in the land of Canaan:
> now therefore, we pray thee, let thy servants dwell in the
> land of Goshen.
>
> And Pharaoh spake unto Joseph, saying, Thy father and
> thy brethren are come unto thee:
>
> The land of Egypt is before thee; in the best of the land
> make thy father and brethren to dwell; in the land of
> Goshen let them dwell: and if thou knowest any men of
> activity among them, then make them rulers over my
> cattle [Gen. 47:4–6].

Since shepherding was not popular for the Egyptians, Pharaoh
needed someone to care for his cattle.

Now Joseph presents his own father to Pharaoh, and this is really
quite remarkable. I want you to notice that Jacob now stands in the
best light in which we've ever seen him during our study of him.

> And Joseph brought in Jacob his father, and set him be-
> fore Pharaoh: and Jacob blessed Pharaoh [Gen. 47:7].

Notice that it is Jacob who is blessing Pharaoh. He is beginning to live up to his name. He is a witness for God now. The lesser is always blessed of the greater, and Jacob blesses Pharaoh as a witness for God.

And Pharaoh said unto Jacob, How old art thou? [Gen. 47:8].

At this point, if Jacob were living by that old nature which controlled him at the beginning, he would have said, "Well, Pharaoh, I am 130 years old, and I want to tell you what I have accomplished in my lifetime. I would like to tell you how I outsmarted my brother when I was a young fellow and how I became rich by outsmarting my father-in-law." And he could have bragged about his family—"I've got twelve sons. . . ." He could have gone on and on. But Jacob is a different man now. Listen to him—

And Jacob said unto Pharaoh, The days of the years of my pilgrimage are an hundred and thirty years: few and evil have the days of the years of my life been, and have not attained unto the days of the years of the life of my fathers in the days of their pilgrimage [Gen. 47:9].

First of all, notice that he was 130 years old when he came down to the land of Egypt, and he will be 147 years old when he dies. Therefore, he will spend 17 years in the land of Egypt. I imagine that he was right on the verge of death—one foot in the grave and the other foot on a banana peel—when he came down to Egypt. But the joy of finding Joseph alive and of being with him in Egypt prolonged his life 17 years.

Again, this audience with Pharaoh is an opportunity for the old man to boast, but notice how changed this man Jacob is. He says that he is 130 years old and his life is really nothing to brag about. "Few and evil have the days of the years of my life been." He doesn't brag about pulling a trick on his old father. Instead, he says he doesn't measure up to his fathers. I "have not attained unto the days of the years of the life of my fathers in the days of their pilgrimage." Isn't this a changed man? It doesn't sound like the old Jacob, does it? He's giving glory to God for his life, and he is making no boast that he has accomplished a great deal.

And Jacob blessed Pharaoh, and went out from before Pharaoh [Gen. 47:10].

Frankly, my feeling is that Jacob has arrived. What an opportunity he has to boast, but he doesn't take advantage of it. Someone else might have thought, *Pharaoh is a great ruler, but I want him to know that I was a pretty big man up yonder in the land of Canaan!* But Jacob doesn't brag—he is just a sinner, saved by the grace of God.

In our day we hear so much boasting on the part of many Christians. Sometimes in our own circles, we attempt to applaud certain men for what they have done. We talk about how great they are. Well, if we all told the truth, we would say that we are just a bunch of sinners and we haven't anything to brag about except a wonderful Savior who has been gracious and patient with us down through the years. He is all any of us have to boast about.

Neither can we say that we are superior to our fathers. A friend of mine, who is now a seminary professor, told me how ashamed he had been of his dad. When he first went off to college, his dad was coming to that college to speak because he was a preacher and a Bible teacher. My friend said he was so ashamed of his dad that he wouldn't even go to the meeting where he spoke. He pretended to be sick so he would not have to go. He said, "I was so ashamed of him that I didn't want to be known as his son!" He spent four years in college and then went into the business world for a couple of years. He said, "I had a rough time, and I changed my thinking about my dad. I had thought he was pretty stupid, but I realized that he had supported his family and had been an excellent Bible teacher. After I had experienced some rough times in the business world, I came home, and my, how my dad had improved! No one has ever learned as much as my dad had learned during those brief years I had been away from home!" He came to the conclusion that his dad was a lot smarter than he had thought him to be. Isn't that same kind of story true of many of us? But it is not true of Jacob here. He takes a humble place because he is a changed man now.

And Joseph placed his father and his brethren, and gave them a possession in the land of Egypt, in the best of the land, in the land of Rameses, as Pharaoh had commanded [Gen. 47:11].

The land of Rameses is the land of Goshen.

And Joseph nourished his father and his brethren, and all his father's household, with bread, according to their families.

And there was no bread in all the land; for the famine was very sore, so that the land of Egypt and all the land of Canaan fainted by reason of the famine [Gen. 47:12–13].

The reason that only Egypt and Canaan are mentioned is because they are the two geographical locations which are involved in our story. If Jacob had remained in Canaan with his family, they would have perished. Grain had been stored in the land of Egypt, but the land is not producing grain anymore. Evidently the famine has spread all over Africa, because the Nile River is not overflowing, which is so necessary for Egypt's crop production.

And Joseph gathered up all the money that was found in the land of Egypt, and in the land of Canaan, for the corn which they bought: and Joseph brought the money into Pharaoh's house [Gen. 47:14].

We are coming now to something for which Joseph has been criticized. People say he took advantage of poverty and he bought up the land. In other words, he closed in on the mortgages and bought the land. I feel that this is an unfair criticism of Joseph. To begin with, he

is the agent of Pharaoh. None of this is for himself; he is making no
effort to enrich himself. He was not crooked in any sense of the word.
He did not gain personally because of the famine.

An illustration of this is the scarcity of and demand for uranium
during wartime in my own country. When some men found that they
had uranium in their properties—especially in Arizona—they were
paid handsome sums for their land. Were they taking advantage of
their government? I don't think so. The law of supply and demand
was in operation.

It seems to me that this same principle was in operation in the land
of Egypt. Joseph bought the land for Pharaoh, and he is enabling the
people to live by furnishing them food. I think that Joseph stayed
within the confines of the law of supply and demand.

**And when money failed in the land of Egypt, and in the
land of Canaan, all the Egyptians came unto Joseph,
and said, Give us bread: for why should we die in thy
presence? for the money faileth. And Joseph said, Give
your cattle; and I will give you for your cattle, if money
fail.**

**And they brought their cattle unto Joseph: and Joseph
gave them bread in exchange for horses, and for the
flocks, and for the cattle of the herds, and for the asses:
and he fed them with bread for all their cattle for that
year.**

**When that year was ended, they came unto him the sec-
ond year, and said unto him, We will not hide it from my
lord, how that our money is spent; my lord also hath our
herds of cattle; there is not aught left in the sight of my
lord, but our bodies, and our lands:**

**Wherefore shall we die before thine eyes, both we and
our land? buy us and our land for bread, and we and
our land will be servants unto Pharaoh: and give us**

seed, that we may live, and not die, that the land be not desolate.

And Joseph bought all the land of Egypt for Pharaoh; for the Egyptians sold every man his field, because the famine prevailed over them: so the land became Pharaoh's [Gen. 47:15-20].

There is no doubt that the famine was a very terrible thing.

And as for the people, he removed them to cities from one end of the borders of Egypt even to the other end thereof [Gen. 47:21].

There was a great migration into the urban areas so that they would be near the center of supply where the grain was stored. You remember that Joseph had chosen these centers throughout Egypt at the very beginning. He now brings the people where they will be close to the supply of food.

Then Joseph said unto the people, Behold, I have bought you this day and your land for Pharaoh: lo, here is seed for you, and ye shall sow the land.

And it shall come to pass in the increase, that ye shall give the fifth part unto Pharaoh, and four parts shall be your own, for seed of the field, and for your food, and for them of your households, and for food for your little ones [Gen. 47:23-24].

Joseph knows that the famine will be ended the next year; so he tells the people to sow their grain.

And they said, Thou hast saved our lives; let us find grace in the sight of my lord, and we will be Pharaoh's servants.

And Joseph made it a law over the land of Egypt unto this day, that Pharaoh should have the fifth part; except the land of the priests only, which became not Pharaoh's [Gen. 47:25–26].

JOSEPH PROMISES JACOB BURIAL IN CANAAN

And Israel dwelt in the land of Egypt, in the country of Goshen; and they had possessions therein, and grew, and multiplied exceedingly.

And Jacob lived in the land of Egypt seventeen years; so the whole age of Jacob was an hundred forty and seven years.

And the time drew nigh that Israel must die: and he called his son Joseph, and said unto him, If now I have found grace in thy sight, put, I pray thee, thy hand under my thigh, and deal kindly and truly with me; bury me not, I pray thee, in Egypt:

But I will lie with my fathers, and thou shalt carry me out of Egypt, and bury me in their buryingplace. And he said, I will do as thou hast said.

And he said, Swear unto me. And he sware unto him. And Israel bowed himself upon the bed's head [Gen. 47:27–31].

I think there are several factors which entered into Jacob's request to be buried back in the land of Canaan. First of all, he is now 147 years old, and he becomes alarmed that he will die in the land of Egypt. I think that is clear to him now. Then, the success of Joseph in acquiring all the land for Pharaoh makes him believe that his family might become comfortable in Egypt and never want to return to Canaan. His age certainly told him that he would die shortly.

We need to recognize this request as an evidence of the faith of Jacob in the covenant which God had made with his fathers. We need to note this because it will come up several times as we go through the Bible. The hope of the Old Testament is an *earthly* hope. Abraham believed that he would be raised from the dead in that land, so he wanted to be buried there. Isaac believed the same. Now Jacob is expressing that same faith. You see, the hope in the Old Testament is not to be caught up to meet the Lord in the air and enter the city of the New Jerusalem, which is the eternal and permanent abode of the *church*.

The hope of the Old Testament is in Christ's Kingdom which will be set up on this earth. When that happens, Israel's great hope will be fulfilled, and these people will be raised for that Kingdom. The first thousand years of it will be a time of testing, and after that the eternal Kingdom will continue on and on. This is why Jacob does not want to be buried in Egypt. If he had no faith or hope in God's promise to him, what difference would it make where he was buried?

For believers today it makes no difference where we are buried. At the time of the Rapture, wherever we are, we shall be raised, and our bodies will join our spirits; that is, if we have died before the Rapture takes place. If we are still living, then we shall be changed and caught up to meet the Lord in the air. So it won't make any difference if we are buried in Egypt or in Canaan or in Los Angeles, or in Timbuktu. The living "in Christ" and the dead "in Christ" in all of these places will be caught up. It won't make any difference where we are. We don't need to go to a launching pad in Florida and take off from there. No, our hope is a heavenly hope.

The hope of the Old Testament is an earthly hope, and the fact that Jacob wants to be buried back in the land is an evidence of his faith in the Resurrection. He hopes to be raised from the dead in the Promised Land. Jacob is now becoming a man of faith.

CHAPTER 48

THEME: Joseph visits Jacob during his last illness;
Jacob blesses Ephraim and Manasseh

This tells us of Jacob's last sickness and his blessing of the two sons of Joseph. We are told in Hebrews 11:21 that "by faith Jacob, when he was a-dying, blessed both the sons of Joseph; and worshipped, leaning upon the top of his staff."

This chapter gives us another occasion to see further evidence of the spiritual growth of Jacob. He has come a long, long way since his early days. We may feel that it is unfortunate that these traits which appear in the last days of Jacob were not present in his early life. But isn't it wonderful to be able to observe in this that spiritual life is a growth and a development! It is not some sensational experience which takes place in a moment of time, but it is described scripturally as a walk in the Spirit. There was too much of the old nature in Jacob when he was a young man, and the new nature is not discerned until he is an old man.

A fine-looking couple in Memphis, Tennessee, had come forward after a service. I asked them what they came forward for. They said they wanted all that God had for them. I found out that they came forward every Sunday. They thought they would have some sensational, momentous experience that would all of a sudden make them fully grown Christians. Scripture tells us we are to ". . . *grow* in grace, and in the knowledge of our Lord and Saviour Jesus Christ" (2 Pet. 3:18). We see in Jacob that we must wait for the fruit of the Spirit to develop. But thank God for the possibility of growth in our lives and for the patience of God which permits it. Also, we can thank Him that He doesn't move in, as we would, and try to force growth. God very patiently dealt with Jacob, and He will deal very patiently with you and me.

JOSEPH VISITS JACOB DURING HIS LAST ILLNESS

And it came to pass after these things, that one told Joseph, Behold, thy father is sick: and he took with him his two sons, Manasseh and Ephraim.

And one told Jacob, and said, Behold, thy son Joseph cometh unto thee: and Israel strengthened himself, and sat upon the bed.

And Jacob said unto Joseph, God Almighty appeared unto me at Luz in the land of Canaan, and blessed me [Gen. 48:1–3].

Can you imagine the thrill that fills the heart of this old man? Here comes Joseph, his favorite son, with his two young boys. Jacob never dreamed he would see Joseph again because he thought he had been killed. Yet he sees Joseph elevated to this important position in Egypt, and he can trace the way God had worked out the affairs of his life. Jacob had been in Egypt for 17 years now. He is an old man and is dying, but he musters his strength to sit at the edge of his bed. Notice that his thinking goes back to the time God appeared to him at Luz, and he says to Joseph, "God Almighty appeared unto me at Luz in the land of Canaan, and blessed me." Jacob has come a long way. We see now the *faith* of Jacob. He is now trusting God. He is not bragging about himself. As a young man he was clever and could get what he wanted—or so he thought—and he would use any kind of method to get it. But now, as he looks back over his life, he remembers when God appeared to him at Bethel, both when he was leaving the land of Canaan and when he was returning. He says, "God appeared to me there, and God blessed me."

Now we see the faith of Jacob—

And said unto me, Behold, I will make thee fruitful, and multiply thee, and I will make of thee a multitude of people; and will give this land to thy seed after thee for an everlasting possession [Gen. 48:4].

Let's pay special attention to God's promise that Jacob mentions, which runs through the Old and New Testaments. He made the promise to the line of the patriarchs: Abraham, Isaac, and Jacob. There are three specific points to the covenant: (1) the *nation,* (2) the *land,* and (3) the *blessing.* But the two important things for Jacob right here are these: (1) "I will make thee fruitful, and multiply thee, and I will make of thee a multitude of people"; (2) "and will give this land to thy seed after thee for an everlasting possession."

The third part of the covenant is important for you and me. "In thee shall all the families of the earth be blessed."

The reason that you and I are sitting down with the Bible right now is because God has made good two-thirds of this promise which He covenanted thousands of years ago. The one-third is still not fulfilled. The Jews do not have the land of Israel yet. Oh, they have a little border of it, but it is certainly a bone of contention. When they get the land from the hand of God, they will live there in peace. Every man will be under his vine and his fig tree. They will own property and pay no taxes. That sounds like the Millennium, doesn't it? Well, that is what it will be.

JACOB BLESSES EPHRAIM AND MANASSEH

And now thy two sons, Ephraim and Manasseh, which were born unto thee in the land of Egypt before I came unto thee into Egypt, are mine; as Reuben and Simeon, they shall be mine.

And thy issue, which thou begettest after them, shall be thine, and shall be called after the name of their brethren in their inheritance [Gen. 48:5–6].

These two grandsons, the two sons of Joseph, will each become a tribe. One would conclude that there are thirteen tribes of Israel, since there are twelve sons, and now the two sons of Joseph are each to become a tribe. There was no tribe of Joseph, but there were the tribes of Ephraim and Manasseh, and that makes thirteen in any man's mathematics. Yet the Bible counts twelve tribes. You see, the tribe of Levi was not counted as a tribe. They became the high priestly tribe and were not given any land or territory but were scattered as priests throughout the other tribes. So they were not counted as a tribe. You may consider that to be a rather devious way of counting, but I didn't do it; the Word of God counts it that way. That is the way God wanted it to be, and so that is the way God made it.

Ephraim and Manasseh are over 17 years old because they were born before Jacob came to Egypt. They each become a tribe.

Notice now that Jacob's mind goes back to Rachel, his beloved, the mother of Joseph.

> **And as for me, when I came from Padan, Rachel died by me in the land of Canaan in the way, when yet there was but a little way to come unto Ephrath: and I buried her there in the way of Ephrath; the same is Beth-lehem [Gen. 48:7].**

My friend, when you and I sing "O Little Town of Bethlehem," we think of the birth of Jesus, but if Jacob could hear us, he would think primarily of the death of his beloved and beautiful Rachel. Here he is on his deathbed, and his thoughts go back to the place where he buried her. That was his heartbreak.

> **And Israel beheld Joseph's sons, and said, Who are these?**
>
> **And Joseph said unto his father, They are my sons, whom God hath given me in this place. And he said, Bring them, I pray thee, unto me, and I will bless them [Gen. 48:8–9].**

Have you noticed that both Isaac and Jacob had trouble seeing when they got old? The brightness of the sun may have something to do with it. Even today there is a lot of eye disease in the Mideast countries. When I was in the Arab countries, I noticed a great many old people who seemed to have difficulty getting around. They weren't entirely blind, but they certainly couldn't see very well. So we notice here that Jacob didn't recognize the boys.

> **Now the eyes of Israel were dim for age, so that he could not see. And he brought them near unto him; and he kissed them and embraced them [Gen. 48:10].**

Perhaps the fellows are a little embarrassed by their grandfather's show of affection for them.

> **And Israel said unto Joseph, I had not thought to see thy face: and, lo, God hath shewed me also thy seed.**
>
> **And Joseph brought them out from between his knees, and he bowed himself with his face to the earth [Gen. 48:11–12].**

It seems that the two boys tried to get away from their grandfather when he lavished his affection upon them.

> **And Joseph took them both, Ephraim in his right hand toward Israel's left hand, and Manasseh in his left hand toward Israel's right hand, and brought them near unto him [Gen. 48:13].**

Joseph is bringing the boys to their grandfather that he might bless them. The one who would stand before Israel at his right hand would be the one with priority.

> **And Israel stretched out his right hand, and laid it upon Ephraim's head, who was the younger, and his left hand upon Manasseh's head, guiding his hands wittingly; for Manasseh was the firstborn [Gen. 48:14].**

Ephraim is to become the leader above Manasseh. Later on we will see that the tribe of Manasseh marched under the banner of the tribe of Ephraim in the wilderness march, as described in Numbers. Joshua came out of the tribe of Ephraim, by the way, and there were many great men from that tribe. It became the tribe with priority—there is no question about that.

Do you see what happened here? Even though Jacob couldn't see too well, he could tell what Joseph was doing. Joseph was pushing the older son to the position of Jacob's right hand and the younger son toward the left hand. So what did old Jacob do? Well, he just switched hands. He crossed his hands and put his right hand on the younger son.

Why did he do this? There is no doubt that he had tender affection for both boys. They were the sons of his favorite son Joseph. He knowingly gives the blessing to the younger, and I think one reason may have been that he was the younger and he had received the blessing. So he passes the blessing on to the younger son here.

This is an interesting principle that runs all the way through the Scriptures. For instance, in the choice of David, David was the youngest of the sons of Jesse. Why did God choose him? God is illustrating for you and me a great spiritual truth. God does not accept primogeniture—that is, natural birth. Never will He accept it. There must be the new birth. Therefore, God does not pay attention to our customs. We say that the oldest boy has the responsibility in a family. Well, the oldest boy is not the one whom God always chooses. That is, God does not choose the natural man—He chooses no man because of his natural ability. How we need to learn this truth in our day! Now don't misunderstand me. God can use talent, but it must be dedicated to Him! If it took talent alone to bring about revival, we would have had revival in California years ago. We have Christian talent all around, but we don't have revival. Why not? Because the talent is not dedicated to God. I tell you, my friend, it must be *yielded* to Him to be used of Him.

And old Jacob crossed his hands as he laid them on the heads of his grandsons so that he gave the younger boy the priority.

> And he blessed Joseph, and said, God, before whom my
> fathers Abraham and Isaac did walk, the God which fed
> me all my life long unto this day [Gen. 48:15].

"The God which fed me all my life long unto this day." He reaches
spiritual heights here, my friend.

> The Angel which redeemed me from all evil, bless the
> lads; and let my name be named on them, and the name
> of my fathers Abraham and Isaac; and let them grow
> into a multitude in the midst of the earth [Gen. 48:16].

"The Angel which redeemed me from all evil, bless the lads." He has
nothing to boast about except a wonderful Redeemer. And they did
"grow into a multitude in the midst of the earth" just as he said.

> And when Joseph saw that his father laid his right hand
> upon the head of Ephraim, it displeased him; and he
> held up his father's hand, to remove it from Ephraim's
> head unto Manasseh's head. And Jacob said unto his
> father, Not so, my father: for this is the firstborn; put thy
> right hand upon his head [Gen. 48:17–19].

Watch old Jacob's reaction—

> And his father refused, and said, I know it, my son, I
> know it; he also shall become a people, and he also
> shall be great: but truly his younger brother shall be
> greater than he, and his seed shall become a multitude
> of nations [Gen. 48:19].

"His seed shall become a multitude of nations"—that's important to
see.

Joseph had better accept this because he is not the oldest, either. He
happens to be one of the youngest, and yet the blessing is given to *his*
sons.

> And he blessed them that day, saying, In thee shall Is-
> rael bless, saying, God make thee as Ephraim and as
> Manasseh: and he set Ephraim before Manasseh.
>
> And Israel said unto Joseph, Behold, I die: but God shall
> be with you, and bring you again unto the land of your
> fathers [Gen. 48:20–21].

Notice Jacob's *faith* in God.

> Moreover I have given to thee one portion above thy
> brethren, which I took out of the hand of the Amorite
> with my sword and with my bow [Gen. 48:22].

That is, Joseph, through his *two* sons, would have a greater inheritance than the other brothers would have.

This apparently was a personal gift made by Jacob to Joseph (see
John 4:5). It was a ridge near Sychar where Joseph was buried. It com-
pensated for the fact that two tribes came from Joseph and they needed
more territory. It was a parcel of land which Jacob first bought from the
Amorite, then later they retook it by force. Jacob returned the compli-
ment, and by force he reclaimed it. It has been an area of controversy
up to the present time. It is here that modern Israel wants to build on
the West Bank.

CHAPTER 49

THEME: Jacob's deathbed blessing and prophecy; final words and death of Jacob

This is another remarkable chapter, as it is the deathbed scene of old Jacob. In fact, in the previous chapter we saw him on that deathbed as he strengthened himself, sat upon the bed, and blessed the sons of Joseph.

After that interview, the rest of Jacob's sons came in, so that around him now are all twelve of his sons. He has a farewell message for each of them. He begins with the eldest and goes right down the list. Anything that a man says on his deathbed is important because generally, if he ever tells the truth, he tells it on his deathbed. This deathbed message is dramatic because it is prophetic. It tells what will happen to the twelve sons of Jacob when they become tribes. What was prophetic then has now become largely historical.

This is our final opportunity to see another evidence of faith in the life of Jacob. He spoke to his boys who were to become the twelve tribes in the nation of Israel and would be dwelling in the land of Canaan. What faith! Remember that the Canaanite was then in the land and that Jacob's family was favorably situated in Egypt.

JACOB'S DEATHBED BLESSING AND PROPHECY

And Jacob called unto his sons, and said, Gather yourselves together, that I may tell you that which shall befall you in the last days [Gen. 49:1].

We come here to an important expression. We find that there are certain expressions which the Bible uses over and over again. One of those expressions is right here: "in the last days." The last days of the nation Israel will be different from the last days of the church. There is a very sharp dispensational distinction which needs to be made. Now he is talking about the last days of the nation Israel and what is going to happen then to the twelve tribes which will develop from his sons and will form the nation.

A friend of mine in seminary (a very intelligent young man who did a great deal of studying) wrote his thesis on the prophecies concerning the twelve sons of Jacob and the tribes that came from them. I enjoyed talking with him because he always had something new to offer. I came to appreciate at that time the marvelous fulfillment there has been of these prophecies to the tribes, especially those given by Moses in Deuteronomy 33.

Many folk talk about the fact that certain prophecies concerning the nation Israel have been fulfilled, and that is true. But we can narrow it down further by dividing Israel into twelve parts and recognizing that God has had something to say concerning each of the twelve. Not only have His prophecies concerning the nation been fulfilled, but prophecies concerning each tribe have been fulfilled. My friend, that makes it remarkable indeed. In the chapter before us we will see the prophecies of what will befall each tribe in the "last days." While some of them have been fulfilled already, most of them wait final fulfillment. I will be hitting only the highlights, but if you want a more comprehensive study, I recommend two sources listed in the bibliography at the end of this book: *Paradise to Prison: Studies in Genesis* by Davis, and *The Genesis Record* by Morris.

Gather yourselves together, and hear, ye sons of Jacob; and hearken unto Israel your father [Gen. 49:2].

Here now is the old man sitting up in bed. I've seen pictures of him stretched out in bed looking like he wouldn't be able to raise his head. But that is not true! He was leaning on his staff, as we learn in Hebrews 11:21. Frankly, old Jacob had been on the go all of his life, and he wanted to keep going. Death is really an embarrassment. It comes at a most inconvenient time, a time when we want to keep going down here. (I have made appointments two years ahead, and I don't know whether I'll fulfill them or not. I accept them with one stipulation: "provided I'm alive.") Jacob found that he couldn't keep going. He was leaning on his staff. He wanted to keep going, but he couldn't. What a remarkable man he was in many ways.

> **Reuben, thou art my firstborn, my might, and the beginning of my strength, the excellency of dignity, and the excellency of power:**

> **Unstable as water, thou shalt not excel; because thou wentest up to thy father's bed; then defiledst thou it: he went up to my couch [Gen. 49:3–4].**

These patriarchs recognized the great subject of heredity that is of so much concern today. Like father, like son. Jacob recognizes that and sees that this boy Reuben is a great deal like himself. "Unstable as water" could have described Jacob in his early years. It was true of his oldest son, also. "Thou shalt not excel." Reuben never did. He never did win a blue ribbon. He won a couple of red ribbons and some white ribbons, but he was never in first place.

There are a lot of folk like that today. They are satisfied and do not wish to excel. I have a preacher friend who is a wonderful man. He could have been an outstanding writer, but he didn't want to be. I think he wrote two little pamphlets. He could have been a great Bible teacher, but he didn't want to be. He just did what he wanted to do. He was satisfied with the red ribbon and never won a blue ribbon.

The story about Reuben which Jacob mentions here is a sordid story. I didn't dwell on it when we went through Genesis because I see no reason to dwell on that. Contemporary literature, plays, movies, and television give us enough of the sordid to make us sick of it. God does not intend for us to dwell on man's sins. In fact, He gives us these instructions: "Finally, brethren, whatsoever things are true, whatsoever things are honest, whatsoever things are just, whatsoever things are pure, whatsoever things are lovely, whatsoever things are of good report; if there be any virtue, and if there be any praise, think on these things" (Phil. 4:8). But God records human sins so that we may have an accurate picture of the human family.

The next two boys are classed together. They were full-brothers, sons of Leah.

> Simeon and Levi are brethren; instruments of cruelty
> are in their habitations [Gen. 49:5].

You remember how they went to Shalem, a city of Shechem, and killed all the inhabitants of the city because one man was guilty of raping their own sister. They took their revenge on the whole town! They should not have done that, of course, and Jacob reminds them of this.

> O my soul, come not thou into their secret; unto their
> assembly, mine honour, be not thou united; for in their
> anger they slew a man, and in their selfwill they digged
> down a wall.
>
> Cursed be their anger, for it was fierce; and their wrath,
> for it was cruel: I will divide them in Jacob, and scatter
> them in Israel [Gen. 49:6-7].

In Levi, we see an exhibition of the marvelous grace of God. It is true that they were scattered in Israel, but this was because they were made the priestly tribe. It was the grace of God that could take a cruel person like Levi and make him the head of the priestly tribe.

It is the grace of God that has transformed us sinners into a kingdom of priests, my friend. All believers are priests today. Among them are converted drunkards, converted harlots, converted murderers. I have had several of them in the churches where I have served. How did they become priests in the Kingdom of God? Just as we all did—by the marvelous grace of God. "Forasmuch as ye know that ye were not redeemed with corruptible things, as silver and gold, from your vain conversation received by tradition from your fathers; but with the precious blood of Christ, as of a lamb without blemish and without spot" (1 Pet. 1:18-19). Then he goes on in 1 Peter 2:5 to say, "Ye also, as living stones, are built up a spiritual house, an holy priesthood, to offer up spiritual sacrifices, acceptable to God by Jesus Christ." Who is he talking about? Those who have been redeemed by the precious blood of Christ!

Reuben lost first place, and Simeon and Levi have also lost first place. The king will not come from any of these tribes. There is another boy who was also a sinner. We will see what the grace of God did for him:

Judah, thou art he whom thy brethren shall praise: thy hand shall be in the neck of thine enemies; thy father's children shall bow down before thee [Gen. 49:8].

"Thy father's children shall bow down before thee." Why? Because the Lord Jesus Christ came from the line of Judah, and it is before Him all will bow.

Judah is a lion's whelp: from the prey, my son, thou art gone up: he stooped down, he couched as a lion, and as an old lion; who shall rouse him up? [Gen. 49:9].

Here is one of the most remarkable prophecies of Scripture—

The sceptre shall not depart from Judah, nor a lawgiver from between his feet, until Shiloh come; and unto him shall the gathering of the people be [Gen. 49:10].

"Until Shiloh come"—Shiloh is the ruler.

This is one of the more remarkable prophecies in all the Word of God. Already we have been told that there will be a seed of the woman. That was the first prophecy of Christ: "And I will put enmity between thee and the woman, and between thy seed and her seed; it shall bruise thy head, and thou shalt bruise his heel" (Gen. 3:15). The "seed" of the woman is the One who will do the bruising of the serpent's head. He will be the One to get the victory. This first prophecy was in Genesis; then that Seed was confirmed to Abraham, to Isaac, and to Jacob. Now it is confirmed to Judah—out of Judah's line He is coming. Also, the word *shiloh* means "rest and tranquility." Christ is the One who will bring rest. Remember that when the Lord Jesus walked here on earth, He turned from those who had rejected Him, and He said to the populace, "Come unto me, all ye that labor and are heavy laden, and I will rest you" (Matt. 11:28). That is Shiloh—Shiloh had come.

Not only is Christ Shiloh, but also He is the One who will hold the sceptre. The sceptre of this universe will be held in nail-pierced hands. In the last part of verse 24 of this chapter we read that from God will come the Shepherd, the Stone of Israel. So this Shiloh is also a shepherd and a stone. When we get to Numbers 24:17 we will find that a Star is prophesied. Think of all that the coming of Christ means. He is the Seed promised to the woman and to the patriarchs. He is the Shiloh who brings rest. He is the King who holds the sceptre. He is the Shepherd who gave His life, and He is the Chief Shepherd who is coming someday. He is the Stone that the builders disallowed but who is now become the headstone of the corner. He is the Star, the bright and morning Star for His church. This is the line that went from Adam to Seth (after Abel was murdered). From Seth it went through Noah to Shem and to Abraham, Isaac, and Jacob, and now to Judah. Friend, don't miss this wonderful fact that God is moving according to a pattern and a program here. This is very important for us to see.

Binding his foal unto the vine, and his ass's colt unto the choice vine; he washed his garments in wine, and his clothes in the blood of grapes:

His eyes shall be red with wine, and his teeth white with milk [Gen. 49:11–12].

Who is this talking about? It is Christ who came riding into Jerusalem on a little donkey, offering Himself as the Messiah, the King, and the Savior. "He washed his garments in wine"—what kind of wine? Blood, His own blood. But when Christ comes the next time, His garments will be red. The question is asked, "Wherefore art thou red in thine apparel, and thy garments like him that treadeth in the winevat?" (Isa. 63:2). At this time it will not be His own blood but the blood of His enemies. This predicts Christ's second coming when He returns in judgment.

The prophecy given to Judah is one of the most remarkable prophecies in the Scriptures.

> **Zebulun shall dwell at the haven of the sea; and he shall be for a haven of ships; and his border shall be unto Zidon [Gen. 49:13].**

Zebulun was the tribe which lived along the coast up in the northern part of the land.

> **Issachar is a strong ass couching down between two burdens:**
>
> **And he saw that rest was good, and the land that it was pleasant; and bowed his shoulder to bear, and became a servant unto tribute [Gen. 49:14–15].**

Issachar was also finally located way up in the northern part of the land. They were the ones who did a great deal of the work that constituted the backbone of the nation. They were the workers, and that is the thought here. We hear a great deal about the silent majority today, that is, the average person like you and me. We don't get on television. It is the unusual, often the peculiar, people whom we see on television and whom people consider to be great. People try to convince us that these are the kind of folk who are the important people. But, my friend, they are not the backbone of this nation, or of any nation. The little tribes, like Zebulun and Issachar, which we tend to pass over were really the backbone of the nation Israel when they got settled in the Promised Land.

> **Dan shall judge his people, as one of the tribes of Israel.**
>
> **Dan shall be a serpent by the way, an adder in the path, that biteth the horse heels, so that his rider shall fall backward.**
>
> **I have waited for thy salvation, O Lord [Gen. 49:16–18].**

Dan is going to need the salvation of the Lord because Dan will be one of the tribes which actually will lead in rebellion. We will see that when we get on in our study through Scripture.

> **Gad, a troop shall overcome him: but he shall overcome at the last [Gen. 49:19].**

This was another tribe that settled up in the northern part of the country. Actually, Dan was the most northern so that when the extent of the land of Israel is described, it is expressed as "from Dan to Beer-sheba."

> **Out of Asher his bread shall be fat, and he shall yield royal dainties.**

> **Naphtali is a hind let loose: he giveth goodly words [Gen. 49:20–21].**

As I mentioned earlier, a fellow student in seminary wrote his thesis on the fulfillment of each of these prophecies concerning the twelve sons of Jacob. I have not made a personal study of this, but if you are a student, you would find such a research very rewarding. Throughout the remainder of the Bible, every person with whom it deals personally comes from one of the tribes of Israel.

> **Joseph is a fruitful bough, even a fruitful bough by a well; whose branches run over the wall [Gen. 49:22].**

Joseph had left the land of Canaan and had gone down into Egypt, but he was still a witness for God there. Later, his sons, Ephraim and Manasseh, would be put in the territory which was Samaria later in history. That was called gentile territory in Christ's day. It was a great place to witness, and the gospel did go into that area. Our Lord Himself ministered there. In John 4 we have the record of His witness to the Samaritan people, beginning with a woman at a well.

> **The archers have sorely grieved him, and shot at him, and hated him:**

But his bow abode in strength, and the arms of his hands were made strong by the hands of the mighty God of Jacob; (from thence is the shepherd, the stone of Israel:)

Even by the God of thy father, who shall help thee; and by the Almighty, who shall bless thee with blessings of heaven above, blessings of the deep that lieth under, blessings of the breasts, and of the womb [Gen. 49:23–25].

The two tribes that came from Joseph, Ephraim, and Manasseh became very prominent and important tribes—so much so that out of them came the *divisions* of the kingdom. They were that powerful.

The blessings of thy father have prevailed above the blessings of my progenitors unto the utmost bound of the everlasting hills: they shall be on the head of Joseph, and on the crown of the head of him that was separate from his brethren [Gen. 49:26].

Note that Jacob is trying to tie Joseph, and the two tribes which will come from him, back to the God of Israel, the Creator, the Redeemer. Why? Well, these tribes, especially Ephraim, led Israel into idolatry. Jeroboam, who led in the rebellion and placed the two golden calves at Israel's borders, came from the tribe of Ephraim. So here on his deathbed, Jacob calls them back, back to the God of his father.

Benjamin shall ravin as a wolf: in the morning he shall devour the prey, and at night he shall divide the spoil [Gen. 49:27].

This is a strange prophecy concerning Benjamin. Benjamin was closely identified with Judah, so much so that Benjamin went with the tribe of Judah at the division of the kingdom. The tribe of Benjamin was the only one that stayed with the house of David.

FINAL WORDS AND DEATH OF JACOB

**And he charged them, and said unto them, I am to be
gathered unto my people: bury me with my fathers in
the cave that is in the field of Ephron the Hittite [Gen.
49:29].**

We see that death to Jacob was not the end of it all. He was going to
be with his people. He wanted his body to be buried in the cave that
Abraham had bought and paid for. He wanted to make sure that he
stayed in that land until the day when he would be raised from the
dead to live in that land.

**In the cave that is in the field of Machpelah, which is
before Mamre, in the land of Canaan, which Abraham
bought with the field of Ephron the Hittite for a possession of a buryingplace [Gen. 49:30].**

We can see how much this man knew of his own family history. I
don't imagine that he was carrying with him a written record at this
time, yet he carried this information in his mind.

**There they buried Abraham and Sarah his wife; there
they buried Isaac and Rebekah his wife; and there I buried Leah [Gen. 49:31].**

It is not so much that he was interested in being buried by Leah (after
all, Rachel was buried up in Bethlehem), but he wants to be buried
where he will be raised from the dead at the Resurrection so he will be
right there when God fulfills His promises to the nation Israel.

**The purchase of the field and of the cave that is therein
was from the children of Heth.**

**And when Jacob had made an end of commanding his
sons, he gathered up his feet into the bed, and yielded**

up the ghost, and was gathered unto his people [Gen. 49:32–33].

It is interesting to see that up to the very last Jacob kept his feet on the floor. He started out in life as a man of the flesh. He took hold of his brother's heel at birth which was why he was called *Jacob*, "the supplanter." He lived up to that name which was certainly characteristic of him. He held on to everything that he could find, and he was always trying to be first. He started out on all fours, and he took what he wanted by any method. As a young man he walked on his own two feet in his own strength and ability. He depended on his own cleverness and ingenuity. He thought he could take care of himself and did not need God. He was self-sufficient, self-opinionated, self-assertive, aggressive, contemptible, and despicable.

At Peniel God crippled him. God had to "break" him to get him, and I think God was prepared to break his neck! After that, he went through life limping. He had to go on three legs, using a staff or walking stick, because he could no longer walk by himself. Here, before his death, he is sitting on the bed, leaning on his staff. Now the time has come. He pulls his feet up into the bed, puts down the staff, and lies down to die. This is Jacob. He has walked a long way through life. He ends in a final act of faith, looking forward to the day when he will be raised from the dead in the land, according to the promise of God.

"These all died in faith, not having received the promises, but having seen them afar off, and were persuaded of them, and embraced them, and confessed that they were strangers and pilgrims on the earth" (Heb. 11:13).

CHAPTER 50

THEME: *Burial of Jacob in Canaan; Joseph allays the fears of his brethren; death and burial of Joseph in Egypt*

This chapter tells of the burial of Jacob in Canaan and the death and burial of Joseph in Egypt. There is, therefore, a touch of sadness about this last chapter of Genesis. We have already called attention to the emphasis put upon death in the Book of Genesis. God had told Adam, ". . . For in the day that thou eatest thereof thou shalt surely die" (Gen. 2:17). Paul wrote later, ". . . so death passed upon all men, for that all have sinned" (Rom. 5:12). The Book of Genesis is a full example of the fact of sin and the reality of death. It opens with God and man in the Garden of Eden and ends in a coffin in Egypt. This book recounts the entrance of sin into the human family but also relates the faithfulness of God in providing a way of life for man.

BURIAL OF JACOB IN CANAAN

And Joseph fell upon his father's face, and wept upon him, and kissed him [Gen. 50:1].

Naturally, he sorrowed. He loved his father.

And Joseph commanded his servants the physicians to embalm his father: and the physicians embalmed Israel [Gen. 50:2].

We know that the Egyptians were quite expert at this sort of thing. We hear of the mummies of Egypt. They had a method of preserving bodies that we have not learned yet today. So Joseph called in the physicians to embalm his father. We don't laugh at a funeral, but I can't help but smile when I think of their making old Jacob up into a mummy, and I am of the opinion that his mummy is in Hebron today.

Remember, it had been his request to be taken and buried in the cave of Machpelah because his hope was an earthly hope. When he is raised from the dead, he will be there in the land with the nation Israel. The hope of the believer today, the member of the church of our Lord Jesus Christ, is to be caught up with the Lord in the air and to go to a place called the New Jerusalem out in space. There are two different hopes, and they are both glorious.

> **And forty days were fulfilled for him; for so are fulfilled the days of those which are embalmed: and the Egyptians mourned for him threescore and ten days [Gen. 50:3].**

It took them forty days to embalm. Evidently there are several processes involved. And we note that the Egyptians mourned for him. I don't think this was professional mourning. I think he had become a real saint in the land of Egypt and was probably respected as the father of Joseph. Joseph was the deliverer, but I believe that his father Jacob was at this time a real saint of God.

> **And when the days of his mourning were past, Joseph spake unto the house of Pharaoh, saying, If now I have found grace in your eyes, speak, I pray you, in the ears of Pharaoh, saying,**
>
> **My father made me swear, saying, Lo, I die: in my grave which I have digged for me in the land of Canaan, there shalt thou bury me. Now therefore let me go up, I pray thee, and bury my father, and I will come again.**
>
> **And Pharaoh said, Go up, and bury thy father, according as he made thee swear.**
>
> **And Joseph went up to bury his father: and with him went up all the servants of Pharaoh, the elders of his house, and all the elders of the land of Egypt [Gen. 50:4–7].**

You can see how this man was greatly respected, loved, and honored in the land of Egypt. This is probably the longest funeral procession that the world has ever seen. It went all the away from Egypt to Hebron in Canaan.

> And all the house of Joseph, and his brethren, and his father's house: only their little ones, and their flocks, and their herds, they left in the land of Goshen [Gen. 50:8].

One wonders whether Pharaoh required that they leave their little ones and their flocks so that he could be sure they would come back. Pharaoh didn't want to lose Joseph because he still needed him.

> And there went up with him both chariots and horsemen: and it was a very great company.

> And they came to the threshingfloor of Atad, which is beyond Jordan, and there they mourned with a great and very sore lamentation: and he made a mourning for his father seven days.

> And when the inhabitants of the land, the Canaanites, saw the mourning in the floor of Atad, they said, This is a grievous mourning to the Egyptians: wherefore the name of it was called Abel-mizraim, which is beyond Jordan.

> And his sons did unto him according as he commanded them:

> For his sons carried him into the land of Canaan, and buried him in the cave of the field of Machpelah, which Abraham bought with the field for a possession of a buryingplace of Ephron the Hittite, before Mamre [Gen. 50:9–13].

You may wonder why Jacob wasn't buried with Rachel in Bethlehem, which was probably not more than twenty miles farther north. I think the reason is stated here. Abraham had bought this cave, and Jacob wanted to be buried with his fathers in a place that was bought and

paid for to make sure that he would stay in the land. So he was buried
with the other patriarchs. They all had the same hope of resurrection.

JOSEPH ALLAYS THE FEARS OF HIS BRETHREN

**And Joseph returned into Egypt, he, and his brethren,
and all that went up with him to bury his father, after he
had buried his father.**

**And when Joseph's brethren saw that their father was
dead, they said, Joseph will peradventure hate us, and
will certainly requite us all the evil which we did unto
him.**

**And they sent a messenger unto Joseph, saying, Thy
father did command before he died, saying,**

**So shall ye say unto Joseph, Forgive, I pray thee now, the
trespass of thy brethren, and their sins; for they did unto
thee evil: and now, we pray thee, forgive the trespass of
the servants of the God of thy father. And Joseph wept
when they spake unto him [Gen. 50:14–17].**

Evidently the brothers had gone to Jacob before he died and had expressed their fears regarding what would happen to them after he was
gone. They were afraid that Joseph would turn on them and be against
them once the father was gone. So Jacob had given them a message to
tell to Joseph, and he was sure that Joseph would not persecute them
to attempt to get even with them. When the brothers do come to Joseph
with this confession, Joseph breaks into weeping because of it. Now
they are repenting because of their sin.

**And his brethren also went and fell down before his
face; and they said, Behold, we be thy servants [Gen.
50:18].**

You see, the prophecy of their falling down before him has repeatedly
come true.

And Joseph said unto them, Fear not: for am I in the place of God? [Gen. 50:19].

Joseph gives God the glory in every case.

Now here is a remarkable verse of Scripture—

But as for you, ye thought evil against me; but God meant it unto good, to bring to pass, as it is this day, to save much people alive [Gen. 50:20].

Friend, God has a far-off purpose that you and I do not see. I must confess how human I am about this because I can't see any further than my nose when trouble comes to me, and I ask, "Why does God permit this to happen?" We need to remember that He has a good purpose in view. He is not going to let anything happen to you unless it will accomplish a good purpose in your life.

Now listen to Joseph—

Now therefore fear ye not: I will nourish you, and your little ones. And he comforted them, and spake kindly unto them.

And Joseph dwelt in Egypt, he, and his father's house: and Joseph lived an hundred and ten years.

And Joseph saw Ephraim's children of the third generation: the children also of Machir the son of Manasseh were brought up upon Joseph's knees [Gen. 50:21–23].

I take this to mean that Joseph was a great-great-grandfather.

DEATH AND BURIAL OF JOSEPH IN EGYPT

And Joseph said unto his brethren, I die: and God will surely visit you, and bring you out of this land unto the land which he sware to Abraham, to Isaac, and to Jacob.

> **And Joseph took an oath of the children of Israel, saying, God will surely visit you, and ye shall carry up my bones from hence.**
>
> **So Joseph died, being an hundred and ten years old: and they embalmed him, and he was put in a coffin in Egypt [Gen. 50:24–26].**

This is the way the Book of Genesis ends. It began with God creating the heaven and the earth, and it ends with a coffin in Egypt. What had happened to the human family? Sin had intruded into the creation of God.

Why was not Joseph taken up to Canaan and buried there at this time? I think it is obvious that Joseph was a hero in the land of Egypt and his family would not have been permitted to remove his body from Egypt at that time. I think he was one of the outstanding patriots whom the Egyptians reverenced. Probably they had a monument raised at his grave.

But Joseph says to his own people, "When you go back to Canaan, don't leave my bones down here!" In Joseph we see the same hope that we saw in Jacob; that is, a confidence that God would give them the land of Canaan as an eternal possession. And they wanted to be raised from the dead in their own land. Joseph believed that God would raise up His earthly people to inherit the land of promise.

The Book of Hebrews mentions this as the crowning act of faith in the life of Joseph. "By faith Joseph, when he died, made mention of the departing of the children of Israel; and gave commandment concerning his bones" (Heb. 11:22).

In Exodus 13 we will see how wonderfully God honored Joseph and answered his request. Moses and the children of Israel took the bones of Joseph with them when they left Egypt.

BIBLIOGRAPHY
(Recommended for Further Study)

Barnhouse, Donald Grey. *Genesis: A Devotional Exposition*. Grand Rapids, Michigan: Zondervan Publishing House, 1973.

Borland, James A. *Christ in the Old Testament*. Chicago, Illinois: Moody Press, 1978.

Davis, John J. *Paradise to Prison: Studies in Genesis*. Grand Rapids, Michigan: Baker Book House, 1975.

DeHaan, M. R. *Genesis and Evolution*. Grand Rapids, Michigan: Zondervan Publishing House, 1962.

Gispen, William Hendrik. *Genesis*. Grand Rapids, Michigan: Zondervan Publishing House, 1982.

Jensen, Irving L. *Genesis—A Self-Study Guide*. Chicago, Illinois: Moody Press, 1967.

Kidner, Derek. *Genesis*. Downers Grove, Illinois: InterVarsity Press, 1967.

Mackintosh, C. H. *Genesis to Deuteronomy*. Neptune, New Jersey: Loizeaux Brothers, 1972.

Meyer, F. B. *Abraham: The Obedience of Faith*. Fort Washington, Pennsylvania: Christian Literature Crusade, n.d.

Meyer, F. B. *Israel: A Prince With God*. Fort Washington, Pennsylvania: Christian Literature Crusade, n.d.

Meyer, F. B. *Joseph: Beloved—Hated—Exalted*. Fort Washington, Pennsylvania: Christian Literature Crusade, n.d.

Morgan, G. Campbell. *The Unfolding Message of the Bible*. Old Tappan, New Jersey: Fleming H. Revell Company, n.d.

Morris, Henry M. *The Genesis Record: A Scientific and Devotional Commentary.* Grand Rapids, Michigan: Baker Book House, 1976.

Morris, Henry M. and Whitcomb, John C., Jr. *The Genesis Flood.* Grand Rapids, Michigan: Baker Book House, 1961.

Pink, Arthur W. *Gleanings in Genesis.* Chicago, Illinois: Moody Press, 1922.

Stigers, Harold. *A Commentary on Genesis.* Grand Rapids, Michigan: Zondervan Publishing House, 1975.

Thomas, W. H. Griffith. *Genesis: A Devotional Commentary.* Grand Rapids, Michigan: Eerdmans Publishing Company, 1946.

Unger, Merrill F. *Unger's Commentary on the Old Testament.* Vol. 1. Chicago, Illinois: Moody Press, 1981.

Vos, Howard F. *Genesis.* Chicago, Illinois: Moody Press, 1980.

Wood, Leon J. *Genesis: A Study Guide Commentary.* Grand Rapids, Michigan: Zondervan Publishing House, 1975.

For additional material on creation, the Flood, and science, write to:

Institute for Creation Research
P.O. Box 2667
El Cajon, California 92021